RURAL CRAFTS IN SCOTLAND

Rural Crafts in Scotland

JAMES A. MACKAY

LONDON
ROBERT HALE & COMPANY

© James A. Mackay 1976
First published in Great Britain 1976

ISBN 0 7091 5460 7

Robert Hale & Company
Clerkenwell House
Clerkenwell Green
London EC1R 0HT

Filmset by Specialised Offset Services Limited, Liverpool
and printed and bound in Great Britain by
Redwood Burn Limited
Trowbridge & Esher

CONTENTS

ILLUSTRATIONS

PICTURE CREDITS

ACKNOWLEDGEMENTS

It would be impossible to mention all of the many craftsmen who have given of their valuable time to assist me in the compilation of this book, but it would be true to say that, without their help, this project could not have been undertaken. Various officials of the Small Industries Council for Rural Areas of Scotland, the Highlands and Islands Development Board, the Scottish Crafts Centre, the Scottish Tourist Board and the Scottish Council for Industrial Design have provided me with much useful data. In particular I should like to thank Calum Munro of the HIDB Photographic and Film Library, Nigel East of the Glenrothes Development Corporation and Miss E.J. Stewart, MBE, of Highland Home Industries, who furnished many of the illustrations, as well as providing much useful information on craftwork in their particular areas.

PREFACE

Outside the four major cities of Edinburgh, Glasgow, Aberdeen and Dundee, the bulk of the population of Scotland still lives in small towns and villages in a rural or semi-rural environment. In these areas tourism has become a major industry in recent years, and in its wake has come a significant revival in traditional crafts. In addition, the principal art colleges have stimulated interest in many other arts and crafts not traditionally associated with Scotland, but which now flourish in every part of the country and have even begun to develop regional variations. The tawdry tartan and chrome souvenirs are still unfortunately with us, but the visitor to Scotland is no longer forced to rely solely on this type of souvenir. A wide range of fine quality hand-made goods is now available, sometimes in salerooms attached to the actual workshops, more often in the craft shops which have mushroomed all over the country, and usually also in the better class of department store in the major cities.

This book is about the crafts and the people who ply them, and it is arranged according to the medium or type of skill employed. For the convenience of tourists and collectors of Scottish craftwork, an alphabetical list of practising craftsmen follows the final chapter, with a numerical coding indicating the products in each case. This listing can be used in two ways – primarily as an aid to the identification of craft products in general, but also adding a new dimension to a tour of Scotland. Collectors interested in a particular medium, such as glass or pottery, could use the list to plan a trip taking in those places where these particular crafts are practised.

[1]
The Crafts in Scotland

The price that Scotland had to pay for being in the forefront of the Industrial Revolution was the rapid decline of its traditional crafts. The urbanization of the Central Lowlands, the Highland Clearances, and many other factors, both social and economic, combined to accelerate the decline in the traditional self-sufficiency of the remoter parts of the country. The enormous developments in rail and steamship communication in the late nineteenth century brought the Highlands and Islands within easy reach of the industrial centres, thus providing a ready market for Glasgow bread, tinned milk and a thousand and one other commodities which could more profitably be mass-produced in the factories of the Midlands than hand-made or wrought by village smith or craftsman.

Several attempts were made to rectify the balance. Unlike the Arts and Crafts movement in England, which marked a reaction against shoddy, mass-produced factory goods, the crafts movement in Scotland had little or no aesthetic motive. The Scottish Home Industries movement of the late nineteenth century tried to foster craftwork in the rural areas of the country to relieve unemployment and correct the economic imbalance of a situation in which a community was struggling to adjust to the exigencies of a cash economy where no such necessity had previously existed. The Scottish Home Industries movement was largely philanthropic and tried to provide a market for hand-woven tweeds and knitwear in Glasgow, Edinburgh and even London. Its aims were severely practical and utilitarian and there was little pretension to art in the crafts which it encouraged. The tremendous upheavals of the First World War and the 'twenties virtually wiped out the traditional concepts of the rural craftsman. The relentless advance of the motor car and corrugated iron roofs made the blacksmith and the thatcher redundant. Craftwork was reduced to aspects of the rural textile industry. Harris tweeds and Shetland knitwear continued as cottage industries throughout this period when crafts in other media had all but died out.

Tourism provided the first real stimulus to a revival of the crafts in Scotland but in this respect Scotland lagged woefully behind other countries. Before the Second World War, when tourism was still in its infancy, nothing was done to provide the visitor with souvenirs of his vacation other than the ubiquitous picture postcard and a few objects, such as the crested Goss china trifles, imported from the Midlands of England. As late as the 1950s this writer recalls a visit to John o' Groats and finding in the tourist shop there no articles of Scottish manufacture at all. The choice lay between crested spoons from Sheffield, thistle-ornamented leathercraft from Devon and plastic-kilted dolls from Hong Kong. Tourists scrambled about on the beach hunting for the distinctive 'groats' or tiny sea-shells but no attempt was made to utilize this local curiosity in souvenir form. I can cite an even more extreme example of the souvenir scene in Scotland at the beginning of the 1960s. In 1961, while serving with the Guided Weapons Range in the Outer Hebrides, I took a party of American troops (normally stationed in Germany but carrying out their annual missile-firing programme in Scotland) to the village store in Benbecula so that they might purchase some souvenir of their visit. They emerged, naïvely happy with Swiss music boxes and German beer steins – of the kind they could have purchased any day of the week in Dortmund or Dusseldorf – but I was ashamed to find that there was nothing even remotely Scottish in appearance (if not in manufacture) that they could have bought instead.

This represents the nadir of the Scottish craft scene as applied to the tourist industry, for even at that time much valuable work was being done by Highland Home Industries to stimulate craft activity in Scotland, along the same lines as the late-Victorian Scottish Home Industries movement.

Highland Home Industries was formed in 1921 and was a continuation of the Co-operative Council of the Highland Home Industries which had welded together the various unrelated and largely philanthropic efforts to market the produce of craftsmen living in the Highlands and Islands. Since its inception the HHI has been a non-profit making organization, operating from its principal sales centre in Edinburgh and a number of retail outlets in the Highlands. In 1914 sales amounted to a modest £3,000; forty years later they had risen to £60,000 per annum and in 1974 reached the £200,000 mark. Today there are more than a thousand homeworkers whose products are handled by HHI, which holds an annual exhibition of Scottish craftsmanship in London. The emphasis is laid on the products of cottage craftsmen, hand-made by people in the remoter parts of Scotland whose skills have been handed down from generation to generation and preserved through a century of pioneering work by HHI and its predecessors.

The craft shops run by Highland Home Industries at first provided a retail outlet primarily for knitwear, tweeds, shawls and scarves, but by 1960 there was a significant output of Celtic silver jewellery, horn spoons, sealskin purses and ornaments and some woodware. Scottish pottery was conspicuous by its absence. The shops run by Highland Home Industries shone like beacons in the dark. The vast majority of the souvenir shops, from Stornoway to Stonehaven, from Wick to Wigtown, continued to purvey their chrome and tartan wares – shoddy, mass-produced geegaws, not always cheap but invariable nasty, and seldom manufactured in Britain, let alone Scotland.

It would be incorrect to deduce from this, however, that the Scots as a race were insensitive to their cultural heritage or that the arts and crafts were completely atrophied. The four principal academic art centres – the art schools of Aberdeen and Glasgow and the art colleges of Dundee and Edinburgh – continued in the traditions of Mackintosh and MacNair and the Macdonald Sisters and even if they no longer wielded enormous influence on the international field of the decorative arts, as the Glasgow School had done at the turn of the century, they produced in the post-war years a growing body of men and women schooled in the disciplines of the potter, the weaver, the wood-turner and the metalworker. These graduates of the art colleges were destined mainly for teaching careers, with little opportunity to practise their skills except in the classroom or for their own amusement. If the country was not yet ripe for a widespread craft industry, the foundations were certainly laid in the Fifties.

At a time when mass-production and the exigencies of the consumer society seemed to be paramount, when the doctrine of built-in obsolescence was beginning to gain ground, there was a healthy reaction against pure materialism and the public (or certain sections of it) began to turn a critical eye on all manner of manufactured goods. This was not, of course, a Scottish phenomenon, and was merely part of a more aesthetic approach evident in many parts of the world. In Britain as a whole there was a greater appreciation by the public of the work being done by the Council for Industrial Design. From the mid-Fifties onwards both the public and the manufacturers became increasingly aware of quality in design and production. In Scotland the lead was given by the Glasgow Design Centre which, to this day, provides a shop window for the best in Scottish products both machine- and craft-made.

While the Design Centre raised the levels of public taste primarily in the field of manufactured goods, such organizations as the Saltire Society encouraged an improvement in the arts generally, but significantly also in the applied and decorative arts, and eventually in the entire range of crafts, by staging exhibitions, organizing lecture courses and offering prizes to craftworkers. The Scottish Craft Centre, with its headquarters in Acheson House in Edinburgh's historic Canongate, was founded in 1952 to stimulate the revival of traditional crafts and to provide a practical outlet for the products of its members. To this day the Scottish Crafts Centre provides a focal point for the crafts in Scotland. It has been largely responsible for raising the standards of design and execution of Scottish crafts. About a third of the craftworkers who apply for membership are admitted, and it has often been criticised for elitism, but in an area where the word 'crafts' is used rather loosely to cover the excellent, the indifferent and the downright atrocious, the Scottish Craft Centre's criteria of quality are only too necessary.

The Scottish Crafts Centre is essentially a private non-profit-making organization. There are, however, two official bodies which, by the nature of their aims, are largely concerned with the crafts scene. The Highlands and Islands Development Board (with its headquarters in Inverness) exists, in the larger context, to arrest the decline of population in the seven crofter counties of Scotland and with the social, economic, cultural and industrial development of the Highlands and Islands. Inevitably tourism and its promotion forms an important part of the HIDB activities and this, together with the provision of employment in even the more remote areas, has contributed substantially to the growth of cottage industries and small craft operations all over the Highland area in the past decade. The Small Industries Council for Rural Areas of Scotland (SICRAS) has its headquarters in Edinburgh and, as its name implies, is concerned with the development of a wide variety of small businesses all over rural Scotland, offering them a great deal of practical assistance. Increasingly, however, SICRAS has come to be identified with the craft scene. SICRAS operates through the Department of Education and Science, and ultimately through the Treasury, in making available certain funds for the development of the crafts in Scotland. Significantly, the foundation of the Scottish Country Industries Development Trust, as it was originally known, owed much to the efforts of Miss Jean Bruce, then Managing Director of HHI.

Help from SICRAS takes the practical form of the Crafts Entrants Scheme which is available to craftsmen operating outside the areas covered by the HIDB. Grants of up to £500 may be made to graduates of the art colleges, or those with equivalent qualifications, who propose earning their living in Scotland by full-time craft-working, in order to set them up in business. Craftsmen's grants, up to the same maximum figure, may be awarded to established craftsmen for up to fifty per cent of the cost of an approved programme which is designed to raise their standards of production and increase output. Bursaries are also available for practising craftsmen to attend special courses to help them develop or extend their techniques, and loans are also available, within specified limits and with suitable security, for building and expansion projects.

Both HIDB and SICRAS provide advisory and instructional services through their crafts officers and other qualified staff. Advice is given on sources of materials, equipment, techniques, layout of premises, marketing, book-keeping and general management. To some extent the functions of SICRAS and the HIDB overlap and in one important area they seem (to the uninformed at any rate) to compete with each other. In the autumn of 1972 both bodies staged their first trade fairs, three weeks apart, and this dichotomy has continued ever since, much to the annoyance and inconvenience of buyers from the South. The Highlands and Islands Trade Fair, held at Aviemore, covers every aspect of trade and industry in the seven crofter counties and is not exclusively concerned with craftwork. The Scottish Craft Trade Fair, sponsored by SICRAS and held at Ingliston, near Edinburgh, is entirely devoted to the craft scene but is open to craftsmen from every part of the country, including the Highlands and Islands. The Highland craftworker is thus faced with the dilemma of either participating in two fairs less than a month apart, in venues distant from each other, or of concentrating on one or other of these fairs and therefore risking the possibility of missing important business contacts. On the credit side, however, these trade fairs give craftsmen an invaluable opportunity to meet each other, discuss common problems and exchange ideas. From the more practical viewpoint the fairs have gone a long way towards solving the problems of marketing craft goods in Scotland – the small scale and limited capacity of many of the producers and the extreme remoteness of some of the workshops.

The increasing popularity of these fairs provides an effective answer to those who might question the need for two such events each autumn. In numbers of standholders and attendance (restricted to buyers) and in the volume of trade transacted, the fairs have grown steadily, with a fifty per cent overall increase in the number of participants and a trebling of the business transacted between 1972 and 1974. More important, but difficult to quantify, is the amount of follow-up business arising out of the trade fairs, but undoubtedly the fairs have been the biggest single factor in transforming the Scottish craft industry. Whereas formerly craftwork was regarded as a seasonal activity closely tied to the vagaries of the tourist season, it is now a full-time, all-year-round occupation, with craftsmen working flat out to supply the growing demand from department stores, not only in Glasgow and Edinburgh, but in London, New York, Los Angeles, Sydney and Tokyo. A significant proportion of the business transacted at the trade fairs now consists of large export orders.

The Scottish Crafts Centre, the Highlands and Islands Development Board and the Small Industries Council for Rural Areas of Scotland are represented on the Joint Crafts Committee, established in 1971 to administer the funds made available to the crafts through the Department of Education and Science. The Joint Crafts Committee co-ordinates policy and administers the assistance available to the crafts from official and other sources. It is roughly equivalent in Scotland to the Crafts Advisory Committee in London with which it maintains close links.

The three principal craft organizations in Scotland jointly sponsor a quarterly journal entitled *Craftwork* (published by SICRAS) which provides a forum for craftsmen and the general public alike with information and comment on developments in Scottish crafts. The magazine was founded in the summer of 1972 and coincided with a significant growth in the organizational aspect of the craft scene in Scotland. Almost by definition, craftsmen are highly individualistic and many people have been attracted into craftwork as an alternative to the 'rat race'. Nevertheless, the survival of crafts in the modern world has demonstrated the wisdom of some degree of co-operation, if not collectivization. Highland Home Industries and the Scottish Craft Centre led the way in providing collective retail outlets and sales points for craft-made goods, but in recent years there has been a growth of crafts centres operating on a more regional basis and often formed as a result of craftworkers banding together for their common good. They range from Earra Gael at Tarbert, Loch Fyne, which serves as a retail outlet for a wide range of craftworkers in Argyll, to the Crail Pottery Centre in Fife which, despite its title, now caters for crafts in other media as well. In the early Sixties the Craft House at Plockton in Wester Ross was a flourishing centre for local crafts, but as the craftworkers turned to the more pressing and more lucrative immediacy of catering for the growing number of tourists, the supply of local products dwindled and goods had to be brought in from other sources to supply demand. Fortunately this question of divided loyalties has since been satisfactorily resolved with the new generation of craftworkers in the area devoting all their energies to their trade.

Some craft centres arise more or less spontaneously, when several craftsmen settle in an area and gradually pool their resources. Others are deliberately fostered from the beginning. A highly successful development in recent years has been the Scottish Crafts Exhibition sponsored by the local authorities and staged at Fort William. Exhibition is something of a misnomer since it is, in fact, a vast supermarket of craft goods open from early May to mid-October each year and all the goods exhibited are for sale. Similar craft supermarkets of a more permanent nature now function at the Landmark centres in Carr Bridge and Stirling; both serve a wide range of craftsmen in many different media, but have the common denominator of top quality and originality.

Apart from the various craft centres there has been a significant rise in the size and number of craft communities in recent years. No doubt the idea of the craft community was inspired by some quasi-socialist ideal of the self-sufficient community ministering to each other's needs. The craft community of the present day is the product of a new concept of crafts, not so much as a living but as a way of life itself. These communities vary enormously in character, composition and viability, from the 'hippie' communies which have flourished briefly in Skye and Harris, where its members dabble in pottery and basket-weaving, to the highly organized and highly sophisticated communities at Findhorn and Kelso. The Findhorn Community operates through Findhorn Studios Ltd, whose joint managing director is a non-member but is, in fact, the community's landlord. Less commercial perhaps, is the Camphill Village Trust's community at Newton Dee, Bieldside, which enables mentally handicapped people to learn useful crafts and earn a living. Others are sponsored directly by the local authorities who have hit upon the modern crafts movement as a way of turning useless or derelict premises to good account. Thus the Far North Craft Village at Balnakeil, near Durness, at the north-western extremity of the Scottish mainland was founded by Sutherland County Council and is housed in a former RAF camp developed in the Fifties as part of Britain's early warning system. The civic authorities of Glenrothes New Town in Fife have recently converted the mews at Balbirnie House into craftsmen's cottages and the former stables into workshops. The Glenrothes Development Corporation have shown great imagination in the preservation of the original buildings which retain an atmosphere of monastic cloisters. Although the great majority of craftsmen will continue to prefer working in isolation, the need to band together to maintain standards within the craft or to bargain more effectively with the retailer has led to the emergence of the Scottish Craft Potters Association, founded in 1975, and this may be the model for similar craft associations and guilds. There has even been some talk of forming a Scottish Craft Workers' Association and though this is still in embryo the rapid growth of the crafts in Scotland indicates that such an organization is not only desirable but is fast becoming a necessity. At the same time it seems likely that combinations of craftworkers on a co-operative basis may solve the problem of marketing, especially for craftsmen in the more remote areas. A lead has already been given by the Harris Craft Guild Ltd, formed in 1972. This guild operates on a ten per cent commission, deducted from the wholesale price of articles produced by its members. They effectively trebled their turnover in little more than a year.

The rural crafts industry in Scotland has grown out of all proportion in the past decade. From being the amateur pursuit of a few dilettanti, craftwork has become a major contribution to the national economy, especially in the more remote districts where the social contribution is as important as the economic. As rural crafts have developed, the craft shops, on which they rely for much of their retail selling, have proliferated and at the same time altered in character. The old 'chrome and tartan' image is still regrettably present, though it has significantly become much less obtrusive, and there is still a great deal of imported ware, mainly from Eastern Europe and the Near East. The fact that large department stores in many parts of the world, as well as the hotels and airports on the more fashionable tourist circuit of Scotland, are now cashing in on the demand for craft products is both a healthy sign and a potential source of trouble. In marketing jargon rural crafts are now a 'soft sell', and this creates the danger that standards may be sacrificed to meet the demand for greater output. Moreover, there are unfortunately too many indications in certain sectors of rural crafts that an element of exploitation is creeping in. This is particularly true of the less decorative crafts, such as knitwear, in which the retailer's mark-up bears little relation to the miserable pittance paid to the knitter. The rural crafts are now well-established in Scotland, but a greater degree of organization will be necessary in the ensuing decade if the industry is to remain healthy.

In the past five years there has been a growing number of local craft exhibitions, usually combined with festivals and other events of importance in the tourist calendar, such as Braemar Week, Clyde Fair International and the Edinburgh Festival. In connection with the last of these, the first Crafts Biennale was staged in the Visual Arts Centre at Moray House in 1974. Pressure of space forced the organizers to restrict the number of exhibits to 170 – fewer than a third of those actually submitted – and in making their selection the organizers were severely criticised for leaning too heavily on the 'arts' side and neglecting the more prosaic crafts. Within its rather limited brief the first Biennale was highly successful, attracting a large number of visitors and gaining much useful and favourable publicity for the crafts in general. Undoubtedly future exhibitions of this sort will be greatly increased in size and scope.

It is inevitable that, while there is now a much greater awareness of good quality, hand-made products, there will always be a market for cheap souvenirs to satisfy the lower end of the tourist market. That the interests of rural crafts and souvenirs are not irreconcilable has been demonstrated in recent years by the attempts to bridge the gap between the craftsman and the souvenir manufacturer. A lead to this was given in 1970 when the Scotch House of Edinburgh, *The Scotsman* newspaper and the Scottish Committee of the Design Council combined to hold a Souvenirs of Scotland Competition. The object of this was to encourage the production of better designs for souvenirs of Scotland, made in Scotland. What began in a tentative way has since become a regular biennial event, with three sections: individual hand-crafted pieces, prototype ideas for souvenirs, and pieces which could be adapted to mass-production. It is obvious that, although the primary object of this exercise was to raise the standards of the mass market souvenir industry, craftwork is now being recognized as having a very important contribution to make in the field of design. Significantly, many of the prizes which have been awarded so far have gone to men and women who are producing souvenirs by hand without resorting to mechanization and mass-production techniques. Even the definition of a souvenir seems to be changing from the traditional trifle specifically produced as a memento of a country or locality, to become something ranging from a minor work of art to a utilitarian object embodying traditional craftsmanship. This is a healthy sign for the future, obviating the rather artificial and gimmicky character associated with so many of the souvenirs of the past.

It remains only to define rural crafts. In the broadest sense the term embraces all manner of products by individuals controlling all the processes of manufacture from raw materials to finished article. Increasingly, however, it is becoming more practicable for the craftsman to work with partially worked materials, and there is a rapidly expanding industry geared to the supply of materials to the craftsman. In pottery, textiles, glass and woodworking it is inevitable that the craftsman must rely to some extent on materials which have been partially processed elsewhere. Few craftsmen are in the happy position of working with raw materials which they have processed and refined for themselves. The type of crafts also varies considerably, from the traditional village artisan turning out useful objects to a time-honoured pattern with little pretension to artistry, to the art school graduate whose pottery has more in common with sculpture and whose purely academic approach has little relevance to the applied arts, let alone the harsh realities of making a living from craftsmanship. The most difficult aspect to define is what constitutes a *rural* craft. With the complete regeneration of Scottish crafts in recent years it would be difficult to speak of any crafts which were completely rural in their origins. Rural they may have been a century ago, but it is to the urban environment of the four major art colleges that they largely owe their survival to this day. In the sense, however, that the vast majority of craftwork carried on in Scotland today takes place in rural areas, the craft scene as a whole may be described as a rural industry. There are a few exceptions, of course, but most craftsmen prefer the open environment of the countryside to the doubtful advantages of working in the cities close to the main retail sales points.

Remoteness and self-sufficiency are ideals shared by many craftsmen, blithely disregarding such practical problems as infrequent communications and high freight charges in their bid to 'get away from it all'. A disconcertingly high proportion of the craftworkers now resident in Scotland are not Scots at all, and while English craftsmen predominate among the 'incomers', there is a high incidence of Americans and a fair sprinkling of Germans, Poles, Czechs, Hungarians, Italians, and other European nationalities. The craft scene in Scotland today is lively and vibrant with the cross-fertilization of new ideas, new techniques and new materials grafted on to traditional forms. It is also a fast expanding industry. In 1972 SICRAS estimated that there were some 700 craftsmen in full-time employment in Scotland; today the figure is almost double and still increasing.

[2]
Bookbinding, Calligraphy and Printing

BOOKBINDING

Unlike most of the media discussed in later chapters, the subjects of this chapter do not have any tradition as a folk craft – certainly not in Scotland. To a large extent, bookbinding, calligraphy and printing have always depended on the existence of an art in an entirely different medium – literature. Of course Scotland is not without its long historic traditions in each of these fields. Some of the elegant gold-tooled bindings produced in Edinburgh in the sixteenth and seventeenth centuries were the equal of anything found in England at that period, but the craftsmen who produced these masterpieces were working for a very select body of patrons drawn from royalty and the upper strata of the nobility. Unlike England, Scotland did not enjoy a revival in these arts in the late nineteenth century. There was no Scottish counterpart of the Kelmscott Press or the Doves Bindery, no guiding spirits of the calibre of William Morris, Thomas Cobden-Sanderson or Douglas Cockerell.

The growth of trade binding in the nineteenth century, and the mechanization of the binding processes in more recent years, obviated the need for hand bookbinding, except for the repair and renovation of antique bindings. There is a relatively small market in Scotland for the binding of periodicals and manuscripts and thus the purely commercial aspects of bookbinding are on a far more modest scale than those in England. Most of the creative bookbinding done today is practised in the art colleges and it is a sad but inescapable fact that few of the students who acquire a proficiency in this craft will ever have the opportunity to earn a living by it. Such decorative bookbinding as is practised at the moment tends to emphasize the art rather than the craft quality, often ignoring the content of the book itself and regarding spine, front and back boards merely as decorative surfaces, much as a painter might regard his canvas. This approach, which has been developing in Britain generally since the 'twenties, focuses attention on surface rather than structure and regards the decoration on the binding as an expression of the designer's art, rather than as an integral part of the whole craft of the bookbinder.

Many of the designs interpreted through the medium of bookbinding might just as well be rendered as wall-hangings or marquetry panels. All too often designers have had only a minimum of training in the practicalities of the craft itself. Fortunately, since the Second World War, there has been an important shift in emphasis in the teaching of bookbinding. Artists trained as bookbinders are now beginning to regard the craft as an expensive medium and follow the 'integrationist' viewpoint propounded by Philip Smith.

In Scotland today, while the bulk of the bookbindings are the virtuoso pieces of students and post-graduates of the art colleges, there are only a few craftsmen working extensively in this field on a full-time basis. Alastair Laing of Haddington, Sandy Lumsden of Loanhead and George Thomson of Balgrie Bank near Leven are producing fine bindings in the modern idiom, though mainly to individual commissions.

CALLIGRAPHY

Lettering as a craft is of relatively recent vintage in Scotland. The monasteries and other religious houses produced their fair share of fine manuscripts in the Middle Ages but such artistic activity was frowned on by the Reformers of the sixteenth century and calligraphy virtually died out. The nineteenth-century revival was in the prevailing 'beaux arts' tradition of that period and was mainly confined to rather florid burgess tickets and illuminated testimonials. Calligraphy probably reached its nadir at the turn of the century, with extravagant flourishes and eclectic inspiration from the art of many countries and periods attempting to disguise the essential sterility of design and execution. Since the 1920s, however, calligraphy has been consciously rejuvenated as an art form, with greater attention being paid to the basic materials and, if not quite a return to the principles of traditional Scottish monastic lettering, at least some attempt to separate the different strands of style and inspiration on which late-nineteenth-century calligraphers drew so freely.

Fine lettering is practised on a commercial basis by barely a handful of craftsmen outside the art colleges. Illuminated addresses and citations continue to provide the bread and butter work of such artists as Avril Gibb and J.G. Jeffs, as well as the bookbinders already mentioned. In addition, however, Avril Gibb produces decorative panels on vellum, while Alastair Laing combines calligraphy with heraldry in clan crests and histories. Heraldic work, including family trees, accounts for the bulk of the general calligraphy at the present time, other than civic commissions.

PRINTING

The decorative printing conducted at present reflects contemporary teaching in the art colleges, with a bias towards lithography, copperplate engraving and etching. So far as can be ascertained there is no evidence at present of woodcuts or lino-cuts being produced on a commercial scale. There is a certain amount of screen printing, but little of this is applied to two-dimensional products such as greetings cards and calendars. A reaction against the mass-produced, polychrome postcards and greetings cards is evident in the proliferation in very recent years of small concerns devoted to the production of black and white postcards, calendars, greetings cards, notepaper and envelopes. Printing is a medium which offers considerable scope to the artist-craftsman relating to his or her surroundings. Thus Derek Riley of the D.R. Press in Cullen has built up a business in greetings cards, postcards and prints suitable for framing, reproducing traditional Celtic motifs and featuring aspects of Highland wildlife. Ronnie and Mairi Hedderwick of the Malin Workshop (formerly on the island of Coll but now in Fort William) combine wildlife and scenery with maps of Highland localities in their calendars and stationery packs. Stephen Gill of the Arran Gallery Press at Whiting Bay draws freely on the scenery of the Clyde coast for his lithographic and engraved stationery and calendars. Though most of this work is monochrome, Ken Lochhead of Gorebridge produces attractive and relatively inexpensive hand-coloured cards and prints.

Prints and postcards are also produced as a sideline by craftsmen working in other media, such as the Isle of Lewis Pottery and Kyleside Weaving and Handicraft of Bonar Bridge. In addition, prints are often incorporated in other articles or adapted to other media. Prints mounted as trays or table mats are produced by Clanart of Edinburgh and A.Y. Normand of Kemnay near Inverurie, the latter using a heat-sealed technique and plastic materials such as melamine in the process. For the deltiologist, tiring of the stereotyped appearance of mass-produced picture postcards, the hand-printed cards produced in various parts of the Highlands and Islands offer something that is new, artistic and original. A wide variety of styles and treatment may be found in the postcards produced by Northpoint Graphics (Dingwall), the Old Croft House (Orinsay, Lewis), Old Rectory Design (Cullipool, Isle of Luing), Studio Seventeen (Balnakeil) or Ann Thomas (Tarbert, Loch Fyne).

[3]

Cane, Rush, Straw and
Raffia Work

Unlike England and Wales, Scotland has no primeval tradition of corn dollies, those innocent-looking straw mannikins which are a relic of the grim human sacrifices connected with the harvest festivals of Ancient Britain. Thus their introduction to Scotland in recent years is largely artificial – though doubtless in time distinct regional varieties, on a par with the Welsh Fan or the Cambridge Bell, will be evolved. At the present time the only major exponent of Scottish corn dollies is Laura Richardson, who also specializes in ropework dolls and various forms of rush work such as mat- and basket-weaving. Otherwise Scotland is conspicuously lacking. The sad fact is that this is a medium which has lent itself only too well to mechanical processes and this has left little scope for the craftsman who cannot compete with modern factory methods of basket-weaving. Moreover the demand for baskets and canework by the general public has declined significantly since the Second World War; and this craft has been more or less relegated to the status of a therapeutic occupation for convalescents. At the present time basketry and canework is confined to a handful of craftsmen in outlying areas. Audrey Finlay of Dervaig in the island of Mull, for example, produces excellent canework baskets and trays.

Otherwise Scottish cane and straw-work is largely confined to the isles of the far north where straw and dried grasses of necessity took the place of timber in the manufacture of furniture and containers. The only wood available in the treeless islands of Orkney and Shetland would have been driftwood and this was too highly prized for house-building to be put to more mundane uses. As late as the twenties straw-work was widely practised in Orkney and the versatility of the seemingly unprepossessing stalks of rye grass was astonishing. The finest strands were woven into a stout fabric used for bonnets and hats; thicker stalks provided the material woven into belts and carrier-bags, or twisted into straw ropes (known as sookans) on a windlass called a kraa kruik. The stoutest stalks were dried and woven into a wide range of baskets, known in Orkney as cubbies and in Shetland as kaishes. Apart from the different sizes and shapes of these baskets, designed to contain peat, serve as nesting-boxes for poultry or as containers for household implements, each island, village and, indeed, individual craftsman had distinctive patterns and techniques of weaving and plaiting the straw.

Today there is a small, but growing industry in Shetland which has revived traditional straw and canework for miniaturized creels and kaishes; these are sold as tourist souvenirs and while some of them actually contain small pieces of Shetland peat they are designed as ornaments rather than as useful wares. Farther south, in the Orkney Islands, straw-work manifests itself in the distinctive furniture which has long been a speciality of Pomona, the Orkney mainland. The manufacture of Orkney straw chairs is still a cottage industry, though the chief producer, Reynold Eunson, operates a small factory which has been in existence for almost a century. Old-style Orkney chairs were made of black cat straw and bent grass woven together on a frame of driftwood, with a low wooden seat and a high, hooded back, designed to exclude draughts. The general appearance of the chairs has not altered over the years, though the quality and consistency of the raw materials has improved. A splendid example of this art was presented to Princess Anne on the occasion of her wedding, and the publicity surrounding this gift has undoubtedly stimulated outside interest in Orcadian strawcraft.

[4]
Dolls and Toys

The craftsman-designer working in this field is faced with several problems, the most important of which is that toy-making is a major industry with numerous mechanical processes which can produce better and more sophisticated dolls and toys than would be capable by hand. The advent of plastics in the fifties, in particular, has revolutionized the toy industry, undercutting traditional materials in price as well as being much more convenient to handle. A century ago the vast majority of toys were hand-made. The more professional articles were the so-called penny toys of London and Bristol, produced in back-street premises in conditions of sweated labour, but even these wooden toys must have represented no more than a small proportion of the total number. The bulk of toys used by children in the lower levels of society would have been home-made – rag dolls and soft toys sewn by mothers and elder sisters, or wooden toys whittled from any handy piece of timber. There was a long tradition in the mining villages of hand-carved toys produced from pieces of pit-props. Bone, horn, slate and twine were all combined ingeniously in the home-made toys of yesteryear but, given the ephemeral nature of playthings and the rough usage to which they were subjected, it is hardly surprising that little of this 'cottage craft' has survived.

Traditional toys and home-made dolls disappeared in the face of competition from cheap, mass-produced toys – first the die-stamped tinplate toys of Germany at the turn of the century, then the Japanese plaster toys of the Edwardian period and the twenties, and latterly the plastic toys of Hong Kong and Taiwan. Even the poorest family could afford such cheap trifles and there was no longer any necessity to practise traditional skills in wood-carving or soft toy making and thus these ancient arts all but died out. They were revived in the thirties for academic rather than social reasons, and practised at different levels in art schools and in the townswomen's guilds and rural institutes. There was a gradual reaction against the slick, mass-produced mechanical toy, engendered primarily by the teachings of educationists such as Maria Montessori, Friedrich Froebel and Rudolf Steiner, and toys emerged which were designed to stimulate the imagination and manipulative skills of the developing child. The teaching of these educationists has influenced the art colleges in their approach to the craft of toy-making. Students have been taught to examine the role and function of soft toys and wooden toys, to strip them of the trappings of convention and return to basic principles. In designing toys greater attention was paid to the qualities of the materials themselves and these were deliberately exploited rather than concealed.

The craftsmen who have begun to make dolls and toys in Scotland in recent years know that they cannot hope to compete with mass-produced articles on the same terms. Instead they have concentrated their energies on specific aspects of toy-making where their talents could best be employed and appreciated. Fortunately there is a growing number of discerning individuals who realise that sturdy, well-made wooden toys have an important educational role. Significantly the hand-made wooden toys produced by such concerns as Dullomuir Crafts, Playstems and the Whigmaleerie Workshop highlight the inherent qualities of the wood, showing the grain instead of covering it with paint, and using polished and rounded surfaces to bring out the tactile advantage of wood over plastic. As yet there is no evidence of a distinctively Scottish character to these wooden toys, which betray the cosmopolitan influence of current views on child psychology, play groups and pre-school teaching.

SOFT TOYS

Felt and fabrics of various colours and textures are not so uncompromising as wood and afford an infinitely greater scope for regional and local variation. Thus soft toys lend themselves admirably to the present craft renaissance and may be regarded as performing two disparate roles – as children's playthings and as tourist souvenirs. Many of the 'bread-and-butter' soft toys come into the former category – the fluffy trolls of uncertain Norse ancestry, the Humpty Dumpty figures clad in kilts and tam o'shanters, and a whole Noah's ark of assorted domestic and wild animals. Collectively and superficially they may not seem to have much to commend them, although the standard of craftsmanship is high and each animal or creature is imbued with its own character. There may be a family likeness in a shopful of such toys but each one has its own distinctive expression, slightly different from all the rest, and it is this quality which endears soft toys to children of all ages. Soft toys for children are now widely produced all over Scotland, from the tartan toys of Spindrift (Troon) to the animals of Cheviot Crafts (Yetholm) and the rag dolls produced by the Camphill Village Trust. Soft toys are also produced as a sideline by craftsmen working in other media such as tweeds (John Barleycorn) or knitwear (Robert Mackie), and conversely many of the soft-toy-makers also produce utilitarian objects in the same genre – including draught excluders and oven mitts.

Soft toys in the category of souvenirs rather than playthings have developed in the past few years. The best-known examples in this field are provided by Mrs O. Macrae of Cullernie Crafts in Inverness-shire who has evolved a delightful menagerie of felt and tartan rabbits known as the MacBuns. Inspired by the success of these creatures, Mrs Macrae has extended her range to include the MacBurrs and the MacDormice, humanoid rodents with a distinctly Scottish appearance. The Macfleece character toys by Moray Firth Designs (Burghead) and the character dressed rabbits of Dalriada Crafts of Campbeltown are of the same type. Several craftsmen are now making soft toys representing animals of local interest, such as Cheviot sheep, Belted Galloway cattle and Highland cattle. This is a field whose potential has not yet been fully explored. Among the other distinctive soft toys may be mentioned Puffcraft soft toys of Inverness, Falkland bunnies of Fife and the somewhat esoteric stuffed mice, octopus and tortoises produced by Rhona Gordon of Nairn.

DOLLS

Apart from rag dolls which belong to the same genus as soft toys, the hand-made dolls of Scotland are seldom intended as mere playthings. The cost of producing a doll by hand and clothing it adequately militates against the craftsman competing with the mass-producers. Instead the craftswomen have concentrated on costume and character dolls aimed at the serious collector. To the casual visitor inspecting the dolls in a craft shop these figures may seem rather expensive, but this is an outlook conditioned by an acquaintance with the prices of plastic dolls for child's play. In terms of the labour involved in the making and dressing of a costume doll they are not expensive by any means and to the discerning collector they offer splendid examples of 'antiques of the future' whose value will increase with the rapid growth of doll-collecting as a serious pursuit.

Probably the best-known of the Scottish costume dolls made in Scotland today are those produced by Peggy Nisbet of Coldstream, Berwickshire. Her historical and costume figures of the Tudors and Stuarts have won wide aclaim and are currently retailed in London and other parts of Britain as well as in Scotland. Although these are her most important work, Peggy Nisbet also produces a fine range of traditional pegwooden dolls and soft toys with silk-screen printed decoration. Historical and costume dolls are also made by Catriona Cattell-Jones of Glenrothes and Ann Scott of Melrose, while dolls with a distinctly Highland character are made by Mairi Fraser of Rothesay, Sheena 'MacLeod of Forgandenny and the Morven Crafts Studio of Penicuik.

Two other kinds of doll have been produced in recent years which could well prove commercial propositions. Jessie Stuart of Keith won a certificate in the 1972 Souvenirs of Scotland Competition with her clootie dolls, a creditable attempt to evolve a distinctively Scottish form of rag doll. Norma Foggo of Lochmaben won third prize in the same competition with her range of ornamental dolls which combined artistry with simplicity – simple cloth heads and stylized costume were grafted on to conical cardboard bodies. While the prototypes were hand-made to retail at less than a pound each, the simplicity of design and construction lends itself to mass-production and this type of doll could well develop into one of the standard souvenirs of the future.

[5]

Embroidery, Tapestry and Needlework

Embroidery as a minor art was practised in Scotland in the sixteenth century. Though it undoubtedly existed earlier, it was largely due to Mary Queen of Scots that needlework attained the highest standards in the mid-sixteenth century. Her prowess with needle and thread is well-documented, though the provenance of the many tapestries attributed to her and her court is less certain. The tradition for fine needlework which Mary established continued for two centuries as an occupation of the ladies in the highest classes of society and it was not until the eighteenth century that it began to develop as a cottage industry, particularly in Renfrewshire and Ayrshire. The industry actually started elsewhere, partly as a philanthropic exercise to relieve unemployment and poverty. The Duchess of Hamilton was one of the ladies of the nobility who founded embroidery schools for orphans and daughters of the poor, but the credit for establishing the industry is due mainly to Luigi Ruffini, an Italian immigrant who formed a needlework factory in Edinburgh in 1783, employing about a score of young girls said to have been between the ages of six and ten. By 1786 Ruffini's workshop had expanded considerably and was employing upwards of seventy girls, despite various setbacks including an epidemic which affected two-thirds of his work force. Ruffini himself was originally trained in linen embroidery and drawn fabric work, but he adapted the latter to suit the cottons which were then woven in Scotland. The resulting decoration had an open, lacy effect which wore and laundered well and was extremely popular in the early twentieth century. Though Ruffini subsequently worked in Dalkeith, Midlothian, it was in Renfrewshire and Ayrshire that his labours came to fruition. Thousands of girls and women, in the towns and villages from Paisley to Ayr, were eventually employed in muslin embroidery, tambouring, *broderie anglaise*, Dresden work and similar techniques.

The finest Ayrshire needlework, however, was that form of sewn muslin known as white work or white-on-white decoration. This distinctive form of needlework, with outlines of double thread and finely stitched fillings, is said to have been devised by a Mrs Jamieson of Ayr who analysed the stitching in a highly complex baby robe brought from France. The zenith of Ayrshire white work was the first half of the nineteenth century, and the christening robe used for the Prince of Wales (later King Edward VII) in 1841 was produced by the Ayrshire seamstress. This delicate craft was already doomed, however, by the increasing mechanization of the Scottish textile industry. The output of linen rose dramatically with the substitution of powered looms and factory methods for the old handlooms and cottage industry. At the same time the great depression of the 1840s, and the migration of thousands of poverty-stricken Irish families to the south-west of Scotland, provided an influx of very cheap labour which the manufacturers were only too ready to exploit. Girls were taught a few basic stitches and patterns and set to work for a miserable wage. It has been estimated that over 20,000 women were employed in what had now become a sweated industry. The mid-century boom was followed by a slump, and the Union blockade of the Confederacy during the American Civil War, drastically cutting off supplies of southern cotton, applied the *coup de grace*. The manufacturers and entrepreneurs who had organized the needleworkers went bankrupt by the score. By 1867 the Scottish needlework industry was virtually dead.

Its resurrection in the present century was slow and painful and it is only within the past twenty years that Scottish needlework has once again attained eminence. Unlike most of the other Scottish crafts, embroidery and tapestry have been primarily urban occupations and are thus, strictly speaking, outside the scope of this book. Here again one must acknowledge the credit due to the staffs of the four art colleges for having imported new techniques and revived traditional ones, and it would only be fair to record the debt due to the Dovecot Studios in Edinburgh where so many of the leading craftsmen in this medium today received their training and formative experience. The main branches of needlework, together with the miscellaneous minor forms, are discussed separately below.

EMBROIDERY

The academic rather than traditional influence in modern Scottish embroidery is reflected in the astonishing range of methods, materials, threads, stitches and types of design which are now in general use and their application to all manner of articles from useful wares and apparel to purely decorative pictures and hangings. At the upper end of the spectrum is the ecclesiastical work combining medieval techniques such as appliqué and stumpwork with sumptuous fabrics, silks and gold thread. Among the craftswomen currently engaged on the embroidery of church vestments, pulpit falls and ecclesiastical panels are Ellen Cunningham of Dumbarton, Hannah Frew of Chapelton, Mary Johnstone of Jedburgh, Margaret MacLellan of Fort William and Kathleen Whyte of Eaglesham. The great majority of these ecclesiastical pieces are specially commissioned by churches and have their secular counterpart in the embroidered panels and banners commissioned by civic authorities. Patricia Bell of Auchtermuchty has extended her work in this field to include smaller articles which are intended for general sale. These include embroidered panels and heraldic work, but of particular note is her application of embroidery to other media, such as finger plates for doors, decorative boxes and even glass paperweights with an embroidered fabric base.

Several of the other ecclesiastical embroiderers have also turned to more mundane subjects. Thus Ellen Cunningham has applied goldwork to ball gowns and evening purses and also produces sumptuous cushion covers, and Margaret MacLellan specializes in embroidered panels and hangings as well as dress embroidery.

Domestic and dress embroidery is manifest in various forms. June Johnston, for example, has taken the traditional east coast goonie, a loose-fitting gown, and transformed it with a variety of decorative bordering. Decorative dress embroidery is also practised by Margaret Forbes of Rosehearty and Nora Porteous of Culross. The more utilitarian wares involving embroidery are relatively elusive, probably on account of the fact that the cost of the labour and skill lavished on them can seldom be recouped if the basic article is competing with manufactured products. Felice Martin of Renfrewshire produces excellent embroidered tea cosies and similar useful wares, but her chief forte is her samplers.

Although embroidery is traditionally regarded as women's work it should be noted that several craftsmen are prominent in this field. Jack Richmond of Newtonmore specializes in decorative panels, both hand and machine-sewn, while Roy Matthews of Leslie has an unusual line in embroidered collages – an odd contrast with his main output of ornamental metalwork and Scottish weapons.

TAPESTRY

Although this term is often loosely applied to any form of embroidered canvas work intended as a covering for walls or furniture, it strictly pertains to a form of decorative or pictorial weaving. In Scotland, however, tapestry weaving has been regarded almost in the realms of fine art rather than the applied arts, far less the crafts in general, and it is mainly confined to artists working in Edinburgh. The influence of the Dovecot Studios run by the Edinburgh Tapestry Company Ltd is very marked, especially in the larger works which are, for the most part, commissioned by ecclesiastical and civic bodies. The tapestries of Archie Brennan, Maureen Hodge, Fiona Macalister, Kathy McFarlane, Agnes Kindberg, Maggie Reigler, Sax Shaw and Dorothy Urquhart are probably better known outside their native country, thanks to the excellent exhibitions organized in recent years by the Crafts Advisory Council, the Victoria and Albert Museum and the World Crafts Council. The periodic exhibitions of tapestries staged at the Weavers Workshop Gallery in the Royal Mile and the Scottish Crafts Centre seldom do justice to a medium which requires a considerable amount of wall space. It has to be admitted that tapestry weaving, both as a craft and as a product, tends to be both esoteric and elitist. There is a world of difference between the douce embroidered wall-hangings by MacDonald Scott of Melrose, for example, and the sculptural qualities of the tapestries by Archie Brennan and Dorothy Urquhart. Outside of Edinburgh there is very little tapestry weaving on a commercial scale. Chrissie White of Dundee produces tapestry hangings that are small enough for domestic decoration, but in the rural areas the only tapestry work at present available to the public is that produced by the Findhorn Community or by Agnes Hamilton and Monica Hardie of Newton Mearns. By the very nature of the craft, hand-woven tapestry is unlikely ever to become a major commercial venture, let alone a sizeable industry, though it is to be hoped that more craftsmen in the rural areas of Scotland will be encouraged to take up this exacting medium.

MISCELLANEOUS NEEDLEWORK CRAFTS

Appliqué and inlay work were skills widely practised in the Middle Ages, but now revived and beginning to make their appearance in the rural crafts of Scotland. In inlay work pieces of material are sewn into the space cut out of a backing fabric so that the pattern can be seen from both sides. For this purpose strong materials such as felt (which does not fray readily) are used especially for counterchange patterns and heraldic designs. Much more common, however, is appliqué work in which pieces of material are cut out and stitched on to a background fabric. Because this method permits the raw edges of the applied fabric to be oversewn or turned in, a far wider range of materials can be used. A variation of this is decoupage in which the cut fabric is applied to the back of the basic material which is then cut away to reveal the applied piece whose edges are secured to the cut fabric with decorative stitching. Other variations include net appliqué, in which the cut fabric pieces are stitched to a net backing, and padded satin work and quilting which can achieve an almost three-dimensional quality. The prime exponent of Scottish appliqué work is Helen Fraser of Muchalls, Kincardineshire, who produces pictorial and decorative panels, suitable for framing and hanging, as well as the more utilitarian objects, such as bags, tea cosies and cushion covers with appliqué decoration.

There is, as yet, little evidence of a revival in the traditional art of quilting which was practised in Stuart times and continued fitfully as a needlework art until the advent of mechanical processes in the nineteenth century destroyed it as a craft. On the other hand there has been a steady growth of interest in two distinct forms of textile craft, both of which had their origins in North America within the past 250 years. Undoubtedly patchwork existed in Britain at an earlier date but little of this work has survived. It spread to North America in the Colonial period and was there regenerated and revitalized. From being no more than a form of 'make do and mend', patchwork was transformed into a folk art in the late eighteenth century and new techniques evolved. American patchwork was introduced into Britain in the nineteenth century and was practised desultorily more because of the need for household economy rather than a desire to create something which was aesthetically pleasing. The more artistic aspects of American patchwork, however, have gained ground in recent years and there are now several craftswomen engaged in the production of cot covers, cosies and bedspreads. The old image of patchwork, as an expedient of the poorer classes, distinguished by the use of large, roughly square patches of uneven quality and thickness with no pretensions of skill or artistry, is a long time dying but these traditional makeshifts bear no resemblance to the work produced by Lady Jean Maitland of Forfar, Nora Porteous of Culross or Guisachen Crafts of Tomich. The best modern Scottish patchwork relies not so much on colour contrasts as on subdued shades and subtle tonal qualities, arranged in pleasing patterns using hexagonal, triangular and circular shapes as well as the more conventional squares.

Analogous to patchwork, as a folk craft which relied heavily on any available scraps of material, was rug-making, in which strips of rag were hooked through a stout canvas backing. Though hooked rugs were produced in many parts of Europe as well as the British Isles it was in North America that they attained the status of an art, with a wide range of ambitious motifs, from biblical scenes and pious inscriptions to purely pictorial designs. Hooked rugs were re-introduced to Scotland from North America in the nineteenth century – or rather improvements in technique, materials and design were brought across the Atlantic to rejuvenate a craft which had become stereotyped and despised. Hooked rugs with artless, naïve but vigorous designs have been produced in many parts of Scotland, especially in the more remote districts, for many years but it is only within the past two decades that the standard of design and workmanship has been raised, largely as a result of the teaching in the art colleges and evening classes. As this once-despised craft revives, distinctive regional patterns may emerge. At the present time the most intriguing development in this direction is the Fife clooty rugs produced by Nora Porteous of Culross. Woven rugs, which are much more extensively produced on a commercial basis, are discussed under the heading of weaving in Chapter 21.

[6]
Enamelling

Enamelling is one of the oldest and most widespread crafts in the world. The use of powdered silicates as a glaze on bricks and pottery vessels dates back almost 4,000 years and was widely practised in both China and the Mediterranean area long before the Christian era. Enamelling on metal was a popular form of decoration in northern Europe in the sixth to ninth centuries B.C. and examples of jewellery and copper plaques with enamel ornament have been recovered from both Celtic and Norse archaeological sites. There is ample evidence that enamelling of a very high quality was produced in Scotland in medieval times, but thereafter it declined and virtually ceased to exist from the mid-sixteenth century onwards. The revival of interest in enamelling began in Britain generally in the 1860s, as a result of the import of fine Chinese enamels to Europe. John Ruskin lamented the dearth of interest in this decorative art and offered a prize for enamel-work, but this failed to generate interest among the craftsmen of the period. The revival in European enamels began on the Continent, particularly in France in the 1880s where craftsmen resuscitated the ancient arts of *cloisonné*, *champlevé, basse taille* and *pliqué-à-jour*.

The principal techniques of enamelling involve the use of *cloisons* or tiny cells formed of wire soldered to the base so that the molten enamel can be poured into these compartments (*cloisonné*); the etching or carving of a motif in the metal base and then filling the depressions with enamel (*champlevé*); engraving decoration on the metal base and then covering it with a layer of transparent enamel (*basse taille*); and a variation of *cloisonné* in which the backing is subsequently removed so that the enamel has the appearance of a miniature stained glass window (*pliqué-à-jour*). These were the principal techniques of enamelling which were taught in the art schools of the late nineteenth century and they might have remained nothing more than academic exercises but for the activities of Frances and Margaret MacDonald who began producing jewellery plaques using base metals such as copper and pewter. As well as the traditional *champlevé* and *cloisonné* techniques, they evolved techniques in which the enamel was applied to the whole surface of the metal, and then contrasting areas or strands of enamel or metal superimposed. Thread and frit decoration and trail enamelling were other methods which they used, in patterns which drew on ancient Celtic and Scandinavian motifs for inspiration. The result was a distinctly Scottish brand of Art Nouveau which paradoxically found more favour in Europe than in Britain itself.

Interest in enamelled wares of this type declined after about 1910 and forty years elapsed before there was a marked revival, this time largely influenced by developments in the United States where the craft of enamelling had been practised since the 1930s. Once again the major art colleges took the lead in popularizing this craft, though the simplicity of the basic materials and equipment required meant that enamelling could also be taught in schools and evening classes and subsequently be carried on by amateurs in their own homes. The result of the widespread enthusiasm for enamelling is a vast amount of rather nondescript copperware jewellery of stereotyped shape and decoration, but here and there the discerning collector or student will find examples of the craft which rise above the mediocre both in the quality and originality of design, and in the intricacy of the workmanship. Probably the best exponents of enamelled copper jewellery today are Joyce Kelly of Braco and John Leman of Dinnet. Mrs Kelly has produced fine examples of brooches, rings, pendants and necklaces using enamel on copper, but of greater significance are her larger individual pieces, including enamelled copper pictures and plaques. In addition to jewellery John Leman has produced a wide range of articles involving the use of enamelling techniques on metal, from small items such as spoons and wine labels to larger pieces such as plates and caskets. Betty Seidler is one of the most versatile craftswomen in this field, working with enamels on copper and pewter to produce jewellery and pictorial panels, but also experimenting with the combination of enamels and *glasmosaik* to produce some unusual wall plaques. Enamelling on precious metals is practised to a much lesser extent. In this field the principal craftsmen include John Leslie Auld of Thorntonhall who specializes in ecclesiastical and civic jewels and decorative items, and Robert Turnbull of Kirkcaldy. Norman Grant of Lundin Links, better known for his silversmithing in the contemporary idiom, also uses enamelling extensively in his work.

Enamelling is a craft which is feasible in the more remote areas of the country and for this reason perhaps one finds that many of the craft-enamellers at work today are located in the Highlands and Islands. Geoff Salt formerly operated a flourishing business in Birmingham, one of the traditional centres of enamelling in Britain, but his interests in mountaineering and love of the open country led him to move from the English Midlands to Achmore in Wester Ross in 1971 where he has since plied his trade under the name of Stromecraft. The range of his work is astonishing, from the tiny enamelled pennants worn as lapel badges by yachtsmen to pieces of jewellery enamelled on silver or gold as individual commissions. While much of his work consists of civic regalia and ecclesiastical jewellery he has also produced a series of enamel brooches depicting in minute detail the various fishes found in West Highland waters. These brooches are enamelled *basse taille* on silver which is hand-wrought and chased. Other enamellers include Lephen Beag Studios of Carradale, Joyce Littlejohn of Tiree and Menzies Craft of Dornoch.

Though metals, both base and precious, are the predominant materials on which modern Scottish enamels are executed other substances are also used to some extent. Regrettably there has been little experimentation as yet with the various techniques of enamelling on clear or opaque glass, in the manner of the seventeenth century German *reichsadlerhumpen* or even of the eighteenth century Bristol and Sunderland wares for which Edkins and the Beilbys were renowned. This omission is all the more surprising in view of the fact that glass is now one of the most exciting crafts practised in Scotland (see Chapter 9). Enamel glazes on pottery are confined to some of the individual pieces by Waistel and Joan Cooper which are decorated with a wide variety of metal oxides, and to the unusual technique of fused glass and metallic oxide decoration which is a distinctive feature of much of the pottery produced by Gerard Lyons of Moffat.

Enamel can also be used effectively in conjunction with other substances, such as hardwoods. Steel tiles and panels, enamelled first in special opaque enamels and then decorated with jewellery enamels, are now used extensively in combination with hardwoods to form traditional cheeseboards, teapot stands, ashtrays, lamp-stands, wall plaques and even coffee tables. Enamelled metal components are also combined with hardwood sculpture and a variety of smaller items such as napkin rings and jewel boxes. Enamelled chess sets are a speciality of Janet and David Miles of the Scarista Studio in Harris, while hardwood and enamel table wares are produced by J. Saxon of Thurso.

[7]
Floral Art

Prior to the mid-nineteenth century an innate love of flowers seems to have been an English peculiarity not shared to any extent by the Scots to whom the task of winning a living from the soil was hard enough and left very little time and energy for the joys and beauties of floriculture. An interest in flower cultivation began to percolate downwards from the landed gentry and aristocracy in the 1830s but even at the end of the nineteenth century relatively few croft or cottage gardens boasted much of a floral display. The harshness of the northern climate was long held to militate against flower cultivation and it is really only within the past forty years that this age-old belief has been disproved. Today the town and country gardens of the mainland are a riot of colour in the appropriate season and even in the windswept and salt-laden atmosphere of the isles of the north and far west valiant attempts are now being made to induce flowers to grow in an alien environment.

Scotland lagged behind England in artistic appreciation of flowers. There is little evidence, outside the Central Lowlands, of interest in the aesthetic qualities of flowers in the late nineteenth century, at a time when flower painting was virtually a statutory accomplishment for young ladies south of the Border, and the craze for flower modelling in wax was at its height. In one respect only did Scottish ladies compete with their southern contemporaries, and that was in the pastime of pressing flowers. This was pursued at a rather jejeune level. Young ladies and children were encouraged to look out for pretty wild flowers during their Sunday walks and these specimens were lovingly filed away between the leaves of books. Subsequently they could be taken out, arranged and pasted on to pieces of cardboard.

The Americans pioneered a sentimental view of flowers, disseminated in many of the magazines devoted to household taste in the mid-nineteenth century, and this fashion spread rapidly to Europe. Discussion of the aesthetic qualities of flowers tended to be couched in language which was as flowery as the subject itself: "Flowers are the Alphabet of the Angels ...

Scattered over hill and valley they speak what no tongue can express: their beauty and fragrance suggesting a world even more beautiful than this."* From this developed a somewhat stereotyped language of flowers. Each species was imbued with some hidden meaning expressing human characteristics. Books were published in great profusion giving the code to hundreds of meanings assigned to specific flowers. The moss-rose symbolized pleasure without alloy, a tulip signified a declaration of true love, whereas a sprig of ivy merely denoted friendship and an anemone indicated that the person concerned had been forsaken.

This complex flower code was used in the composition of bouquets exchanged by lovers, but it was also applied assiduously to the arrangement of dried flower collages. In their endeavours to convey the most expressive message the young ladies who laboured over these flower pictures tended to neglect the artistic requisites of balance and restraint. Thus late-Victorian and Edwardian flower pictures, like so much else of that period, were fussy and over-ornamented. The First World War, which took the sentiment out of life, killed the fashion for pressed flower pictures. Interest in dried flowers in the inter-war period was largely botanical and it is only within the past two decades that the artistic aspects of dried flower arrangement have been revived. Shorn of its Victorian amorous connotations, floral art has now been allowed to develop according to artistic criteria, with emphasis on line and form, the balance of shapes and colours and the subtle exploitation of tints and shades to achieve a balanced composition. The preparation of flowers, ferns and grasses is also much more scientific nowadays, ably assisted by a wealth of flower presses and other specialized equipment. The availability of better adhesives and basic materials has also achieved more satisfactory results. In this way, dried flower arrangement has been raised from the idle pastime of young ladies to the status of an art form in its own right. It is now widely taught in schools and evening classes and has become a universal hobby of young and old alike. Because the rudimentary elements of floral art are simple and the materials relatively inexpensive and easy to obtain, it has become the most widely practised of the minor arts, probably even surpassing watercolour painting in popularity. For that reason, however, there is a very wide range of quality to be found in pressed flower pictures. The

*Francis Lichten in *Decorative Arts of Victoria's Era* (1950).

forlorn, sticky confections which are a distressing feature of some church fêtes and school bazaars are mute witness to the misplaced enthusiasm of their makers. The fact that they are there in a good cause is little consolation or compensation for their tawdry or trivial nature.

To be sure, there are plenty of examples of floral pictures which are worthy of consideration and bear evidence of the painstaking skill, ingenuity and artistic sensitivity of their designers and it is these better examples which find their way into the craft shops. It might be argued that an art in which everyone can dabble is hardly likely to attract a big demand from the public, but nevertheless there seems to be a ready market for floral compositions of outstanding appearance. The foremost exponent of floral art in Scotland today is Jean Jack of Inverness, who specializes in traditional pressed flower pictures with metal and wood frames suitable for wall adornment. C. Thompson of Greenock also produces pressed flower pictures on a commercial scale, as do Fynecraft of Otter Ferry who also adapt dried flowers for incorporation in paperweights and plaques using acrylic substances. By and large, the floral materials used are the same as those in England, but a good example of characteristically Scottish material is provided by the Scottish White Heather Farm, near Dunoon, who use heather in pictures and small ornaments.

Among the minor arts of the late nineteenth century may be mentioned the use of such unlikely materials as seaweed, onion skins and leaf skeletons to produce pictorial effects. These substances have likewise been revived in recent years and are amalgamated with pine cones and needles, flower stalks, seed-pods and even small pieces of driftwood in natural collages. Dried ferns and leaves, particularly of the rowan or mountain ash which produce an enormous range of autumnal hues, are also used to create pictures, but in addition have been adapted to decorate small boxes, plaques, table mats and stands. The ferns and leaves are applied to wood surfaces and then varnished. Though traditional varnishes are still widely used, modern materials such as polyester resin and acrylic have transformed this craft and made practical the application of floral and fern ornament to objects subject to fairly rough usage. This is a craft which is still in its infancy, but judging by the number of craftsmen exhibiting flowercraft at the annual trade fairs each year it is one which is expanding rapidly.

[8]

Furniture

The death and resurrection of traditional crafts in Scotland are best illustrated by the history of Scottish furniture and cabinet-making. To begin with, furniture was not a medium for which Scottish craftsmen were ever noted. Paucity of proper materials, especially yew and oak, hardly encouraged the growth of a native furniture industry. The chairs, tables, stools, dressers and beds produced in late medieval times had a certain naïve vigour about them. What they lacked in elegance and refinement they made up for in robustness. Carved backs, legs and finials were virtually unknown outside Fife and the Lothians, where the influence of Flemish craftsmen had a significant impact. Furniture was never regarded as an applied art; it was always severely functional in appearance, but this probably saved it from the worst excesses of the baroque and rococo which marred so much of the furniture produced in England and Europe in the eighteenth century.

By the beginning of the nineteenth century, however, the indigenous furniture industry had virtually died out, unable to compete with the cheaper and more satisfactory products of the English cabinet-makers. The increased mechanization of the trade from 1830 onwards finally killed the craft of furniture-making, even in the remotest districts. It is significant that the distinctive Orkney chair (referred to it in Chapter 3) did not develop until the closing years of the nineteenth century, though it was undoubtedly based on a much older tradition. With their intensely materialist outlook the Victorians had little use for hand-crafted furniture when machinery would produce the same article more cheaply and more efficiently. What they overlooked, however, was the innate quality of hand-made furniture, embodying the craftsman's feel for the materials. Here and there attempts were made to revive furniture-making as a craft and the distinctive whitewood furniture designed by Charles Rennie Mackintosh is a superb example of this. Unfortunately, much of the craftsman furniture of the turn of the century was designed for specific settings and did not look so well when removed from its original environment. Cabinet-making as an industry rather than as a craft flourished on a modest scale in Scotland in the early years of this century, but the styles slavishly followed the pattern set by English designers and much of the more expensive furniture reproduced antique forms with varying degrees of success.

It would not be correct to speak of a revival of furniture as a craft, but rather of a rebirth, conceived at an academic level in the art and technical colleges. Moreover, many of the craftsmen now engaged in this trade have come into Scotland in recent years, bringing with them new ideas and techniques. Craft furniture of the present day may thus be divided into two categories; traditional and modern.

TRADITIONAL STYLES

The Orkney chair is the best example of traditional Scottish furniture but, no doubt inspired by the success of Orcadian furniture in recent years, other forms have been revived. Not surprisingly, the more distinctive styles belong to the far north-east where the Norse influence remains strong – as in Orkney and Shetland. Ironically the centre of 'traditional' Scottish furniture today is an area where trees are conspicuous by their absence! John Crowe of Thurso specializes in the smaller items such as hand-carved stools and spinning wheels scaled down to half-size. In the same town Caithness Chairs of Traill Street produce the larger articles, such as rockers and spinning-chairs in the traditional Caithness pattern. This company also makes scaled-down versions suitable for children and a wide range of stools – cutty-stools, dram-stools and milking-stools based on traditional Scottish designs. Alexander Sutherland, of Haster near Wick, also produces spinning stools and dram-stools, but specializes in larger items such as monk's benches and hand-made refectory tables in the tradition of Scottish functionalism. Farther south, Pitteuchar Woodcraft of Glenrothes are making round padded stools and the curious thistle-shaped stools which were a Fife speciality. Haldane and Company of Strathmiglo in Fife produce spinning chairs in the traditional Hebridean style. Other companies, notably Highland Charm Furniture of Inverness and Starfish Design of Fort William, are in the process of grafting traditional design elements on to furniture suitable for the modern interior.

SPINNING WHEELS

Although most of the wool used by the Scottish handloom
weavers today is carded and spun mechanically, often being sent
to the mainland for processing, the age-old methods of spinning
the yarn are still to be found. Not so long ago I was given a
demonstration of hand-spinning by a lady in the Lochcarnan
district of South Uist, using the distaff and spindle. This was the
primitive method which required great skill and deftness to
achieve yarn of even thickness and consistency, but it had the
advantage of allowing the spinner to spin at any time or place.
Far less mobile, though producing better results, was the spinning
wheel which in Scotland came into widespread usage in the
sixteenth century. The earliest wheels consisted of a plain, large
fly-wheel geared to a spindle set in a wooden mounting. The
disadvantage of this 'muckle wheel' was that the spinner had to
retreat from the wheel as the wool or flax was spun into thread.
When a sizeable length of yarn had been spun the spinner would
stop, retrace her steps and wind up the thread.

Spinning was revolutionized by the English, with the
introduction of the more compact bobbin and flyer type of wheel
which automatically wound the thread on to a bobbin. As the
wheel was operated by a treadle instead of being rotated by hand
it enabled the spinner to control the movement and flow of the
yarn more carefully and produce thread of more consistent
quality. In the aftermath of the Jacobite Rebellion of 1715 the
redcoats built roads through the Highlands and established
spinning schools – or rather reinforced those which had been
established after the Union in 1707. This was one of the more
enlightened measures in the pacification of the Highlands and it is
from this period that the spinning wheel became an indispensable
piece of furniture in every croft and cottage. During the two
centuries in which spinning wheels were commonplace, many
different types were evolved, varying in the size of the fly-wheel
and in the arrangement or juxtaposition of the bobbin and flyer.
The usual arrangement was to have the bobbin and flyer behind
the fly-wheel but in the northeast and the islands to the far north
of Scotland an upright form was preferred. Stylistically spinning
wheels varied considerably, from those with simple pegged
boards and plain wheels to those with elaborately turned spokes
and highly polished surfaces.

Although the earliest treadle wheels were of English origin the
production of spinning wheels quickly became a local industry
and most towns and villages on the mainland, and many in the

islands, had wheelwrights specializing in their manufacture. Well into the present century, for example, there was a craftsman at Bunessan on the island of Mull whose wheels were exported to other parts of the Hebrides, as far afield as St Kilda. When the St Kildans abandoned their lonely island in 1930 they took their spinning wheels with them, to Morvern and Fife where they were re-settled, but in more recent years, when people have abandoned their crofts and drifted to the mainland, the spinning wheels were left behind, perhaps to symbolize an old way of life that was fast disappearing in the jet age. Very little hand-spinning is carried on in the islands today, since mechanical processes do the job more quickly and efficiently and the end-product does not in any sense detract from the fine hand-woven tweeds. Hand-spinning might well have gone the way of other ancient skills, and the spinning wheel been relegated to museums along with the distaff and spindle, but for the general renaissance in traditional crafts. In recent years there has been a marked revival of interest in hand-spinning as a hobby, and its devotees will confirm that there is nothing more satisfying than gathering wool from the moors, dykes, fences, and hedgerows, washing and carding it, and then spinning it into fine yarn suitable for knitting.

Because so many of them were fine examples of the wood-turner's craft, nineteenth-century spinning wheels have long been prized as decorative antiques which, like copper warming pans, have enjoyed a new lease of life as ornaments long after their original function has disappeared. Now, however, there is a real demand for spinning wheels intended for actual use and this, as well as the continuing demand for 'ornamental' spinning wheels, has stimulated the revival of a craft geared to their manufacture. In the period between the world wars when the Celtic romanticism engendered by the writings of Fiona MacLeod and Alastair Alpin MacGregor was at its height, there was a certain amount of fakery in spinning wheels. At first, parts from genuine but long-discarded wheels were 'cannibalized' to produce something that looked authentic, but latterly reproductions which would have been quite useless in practice were produced purely as ornaments. This unfortunate state of affairs has fostered a great deal of snobbery, leading otherwise discerning people to reject out of hand modern spinning wheels just because they lack the patina, wear and woodworm of the old.

For the record, however, it ought to be stated that the

craftsmen engaged in the production of spinning wheels today are turning out better and more accurate articles than the majority of their eighteenth- and nineteenth-century predecessors ever did. The spinning wheels of the present day are both precision instruments and ornaments of great beauty, a delight to use and a joy to behold. Haldane and Company of Strathmiglo produce excellent examples of both main types: the Hebridean (tandem) and Shetland (upright) spinning wheels. Harry Pouncey of Moniaive in Dumfriesshire is a third-generation craftsman making 'working' wheels in the best tradition. Both he and John Kearns of Newtonmore also produce pieces of furniture, though spinning wheels are probably the most important aspect of their work. Though Kearns' wheels are in full working order, he has compromised to some extent with the exigencies of the tourist market by offering wheels which are wired for use as lamp standards.

MODERN STYLES

Occupying a position between the traditional and modern styles of hand-made furniture are the craftsmen who concentrate on reproductions, mainly of Georgian furniture in what used to be termed 'country styles'. Hand-made furniture of this sort is produced by Connoisseur Reproductions of Markinch. The most promising development of recent years, however, has been the emergence of cabinet-makers who are designing and producing a furniture that is both distinctively Scottish and in the modern idiom. Grant McPherson of Caledonian Hardwoods in Renfrewshire produces modern furniture from home-grown hardwoods. Norman Ingram of Keith in Banffshire specializes in coffee tables but also makes other modern pieces. Several of the craftsmen mentioned in connection with traditional styles are also experimenting with new forms. John Kearns uses Scottish timbers – pine, beech, elm, oak, ash, birch and sycamore – in the manufacture of coffee tables, kitchen equipment and cottage furniture. Both Pitteuchar Woodcraft of Fife and Starfish Designs of Inverness-shire combine traditional and modern styles in their current output. Nevertheless, there is a feeling that there is still ample scope for expansion in this particular craft, as the demand for fine, hand-made furniture grows. There must be many old-time craftsmen up and down the country producing hand-made pieces as a sideline to their machine-made products and Jenni Hodge, organizer of the first Craft biennale in 1974, recently posed the question 'Where have all the cabinet-makers gone?'

More specifically, Robert Clark, of the Scottish Design Centre in Glasgow, has made a plea (in the summer 1974 issue of *Craftwork*) for attention to be focussed on the crafts relating to repair and restoration. Much of the expertise in this field belongs to craftsmen of an earlier generation and there is a very real fear that this knowledge will gradually disappear as these craftsmen die out. Although this applies primarily to furniture there are other fields in which preservation and conservation of existing pieces is essential. Clark has therefore urged the craftsmen of today to think in terms of 'current' projects as much as involving themselves in the rejuvenating of manufactures by their forbears in the crafts. Ideally, perhaps, a blend of the two should be the ultimate aim of the craftsman; while a regard for the things of the past is laudable it is important that techniques should not be allowed to stagnate and become stereotyped. The problem of striking the right balance is one which applies to furniture-making more than to any other craft in Scotland today.

The associated woodcrafts of turning, carving and modelling are discussed separately in Chapter 22.

[9]

Glass

The manufacture of glass in Scotland is almost as old as it is in England, and dates from 1610 when King James IV granted a patent to Sir George Hay, who founded a glass-house at Wemyss in Fife. This pioneer glassworks exploited the abundant raw materials of the locality, the silicates from sand and potash from seaweed, as well as the rich coal deposits which were then being opened up. Hay imported Flemish and Italian craftsmen to teach glass-blowing techniques to the Scots, but there is some evidence to suggest that he also induced English glassworkers to come north, to the annoyance of Sir Robert Mansell who held the monopoly of glass-making in England. Following Hay's death Mansell secured control of the Scottish glass industry though the monopoly was frequently infringed by other entrepeneurs, such as William Morrison of Prestonpans who pioneered the Scottish mirror industry, based on the techniques practised in the Low Countries. In the mid-seventeenth century a glassworks was founded at Leith and this became the centre of a glass industry which, to this day, is based on Edinburgh. Verreville ('glass town') was founded near Glasgow a century later and though it is better remembered today for its pottery, it soon built up a lucrative trade with the American colonies, supplying them with table glass and other useful wares.

Scottish glass followed much the same pattern as its English counterpart, being affected by the successive Glass Excise Acts of 1745, 1777 and 1781, which had a great influence on the style of glassware produced. The increase in the duty on glass imposed in 1745 led to the abandonment of the traditional heavy flint glassware and the development of lighter forms, best exemplified by the elegant drinking glasses of the late eighteenth century, with intricate air twist and opaque spiral stems. This was also the period when so-called Jacobite glasses were popular, though it is a matter of conjecture how many of these glasses, with their Jacobite portraits, symbols and inscriptions, were actually engraved in Scotland.

During the nineteenth century glass production in Scotland became increasingly mechanized. Domestic and industrial glassware became more functional in design, while the ornamental wares suffered not only from the excesses of ornament to which the Victorians were prone, but was affected by the vogue for pseudo-Celtic motifs and shapes. The development of pressed and moulded glass techniques in the nineteenth century merely exacerbated the situation and encouraged the proliferation of hideous thistle goblets and execrable decanters. Technically Scottish glass of this period was still of a very high standard, and here and there were isolated though outstanding examples of copper-wheel engraving, acid-etching and cameo glass-carving which redeemed the mediocre quality of design in general.

The revival of Scottish glass as a craft began shortly after the First World War, mainly due to the activities of the Ysart family of which more will be said under the heading of 'Paperweights'. The late Professor Turner, founder of the Institute of Glass Technology, played a vital part in the revival of interest in glass in the 1930s, but credit for transforming glass from a craft into an art must go to his wife, Helen Monro Turner who was instrumental in establishing the glass department at the Edinburgh College of Art in 1940. Under her expert tutelage the students of Edinburgh College learned the various techniques of decorating glass and this explains the resurgence of this art in recent years. Outside the great industrial glassworks of the Central Lowlands glass is now being manufactured in several small glass-houses in Oban, Perthshire and Caithness, and by several glassblowers in other parts of the country. The renaissance of Scottish glass over the past decade has placed Scotland in the forefront of the industry in Britain today and its products are recognized internationally alongside the more traditional exports of tweeds and knitwear.

TABLEWARES

Outside the Edinburgh and Glasgow area the bulk of the domestic glassware produced in Scotland today is concentrated in several small glass-houses in the Highlands. Perth became a glass-making centre after the First World War when Paul Ysart and his brothers moved from Edinburgh (where they had been employed with the Leith Flint and Glass Works) and began production of hand-blown articles. Since they specialized in paperweights and millefiori articles their activities are discussed later in this chapter. The direct descendant of the original Ysart enterprise was the Strathearn Glass Company, established in 1964, which moved from Perth to Crieff and has since established a world-wide reputation for hand-blown table glass in addition to engraved crystal and paperweights. Farther north the Sinclairs of Caithness founded a glass-making business at Harrowhill in Wick in the late 1950s, originally importing Italian craftsmen to teach the technique of glass-blowing to local workers. Today Caithness Glass, and its allied company, Oban Glass, are noted all over the world for their wide range of domestic wares, including dishes and bowls, goblets, beakers and drinking glasses, decanters and vases. These glass-houses are equally versatile in clear colourless and translucent coloured glass, though Oban's particular speciality is a clear, colourless glass with coloured striations of a very distinctive appearance. Both glass-houses permit visitors to walk round (indeed, they welcome them) and see the various processes involved in glass-blowing and the forms of decoration employed on the completed article.

Apart from the three glass factories in the Highlands, there are several craftsmen operating small studio glass-houses. As the teaching of glass-making (as opposed to glass decoration) is a relatively new development in the Edinburgh College of Art it is hardly surprising that the bulk of the craftsmen glass-blowers hail from other parts of the world. John Airlie of Kirkhill Glass in Gorebridge, Midlothian is one of the few native Scots in the forefront of this craft, his hollow wares being distinguished by their delicate shades of green and blue translucent glass. Peter Layton, working in Morar on the north-west coast of Scotland, trained as a potter and ceramic sculptor and had previously worked in England and the Untied States before establishing the first glass studio in Scotland in 1970. Although glass is a relatively new venture for him he has already established an international reputation in this medium. His training in ceramics and his cosmopolitan outlook are reflected in his glassware; he often uses sculptural designs and experiments with bold colours, opaque glass and metallic lustre effects.

Both Airlie and Layton produce the more decorative forms of tableware, particularly vases, bowls and flasks, but Ron Boyco of Craggan Mill has so far concentrated on the more useful wares such as decanters and wine glasses. Boyco is one of the two Americans who have left an indelible mark on Scottish glassware in recent years. Much of his high quality hand-blown crystal has the heavy foot rim, baluster stem and bucket or ogee bowls which distinguished Scottish glass before the coming of the eighteenth century excise acts, yet they combine with these features the elegant, streamlined qualities which characterize the best in modern design.

ORNAMENTAL WARES

Because hand-made glass is expensive compared with the run of the mill table wares produced under factory conditions in the glassworks of the Lowlands and England, craftsmen working in this medium naturally concentrate on the more decorative pieces. Glassware as an art rather than as a craft is a fairly new concept in Scotland and it is only recently that the public have become accustomed to thinking of glass in the same context as sculpture and the fine arts, though this idea has long been established on the continent of Europe. Peter Layton and John Airlie both excel in purely decorative pieces and sculptural glass and produce individual masterpieces to commission. Ed Iglehart, the other American working in this medium, has so far devoted all his energies to purely decorative glassware, ornamental perfume bottles and vases. Iglehart trained as a research chemist and came to Scotland in 1972 where he established his studio at Palnackie in Galloway. His sculptural pieces, especially a set of wind chimes in tall, slender glass, excited favourable comment at the Glass in Scotland Exhibition held the same year, and since then he has gone on to experiment with colours and surface effects. His exploration of colour betrays his scientific training and this is evident in the shapes which he has evolved. There is something molecular in the structure of his ultra-modern· chandeliers composed of rods and spheres. Because he is largely self-taught he has brought startling originality to bear on his work and has devised new techniques of layering various colours with clear, colourless glass and using metallic oxides to create iridescent or opalescent effects. Some of his most recent work involves trails of coloured glass, an exceedingly difficult technique to master, and the resulting surface decoration is reminiscent of the favrile glass of his compatriot, Louis Comfort Tiffany, at the turn of the century. He has gone further than most other craftsmen in exploring ways of utilizing local materials — silica from the sands of the Dee estuary, and lead oxides from the galeniferous deposits in the old mine workings of nearby Castle Douglas; he uses an

oxypropane torch fuelled by methane extracted from chicken
manure. This experiment in self-sufficient craftsmanship is still in
its infancy and it remains to be seen whether Ed Iglehart will be
able to realize the dream cherished by many of his fellow
workers.

ENGRAVED GLASS

Engraving on glass was a craft in which Scottish artists
traditionally excelled, if the decorated goblets and glasses, bowls
and vases of the eighteenth century are anything to go by. Even
in the mid-nineteenth century glass-engraving of a high quality
was still being practised in the Edinburgh area, despite the almost
universal penchant for cut glass and eventually for pressed glass.
The popularity of pressed and moulded glass around the turn of
the century, together with cameo glass (imported from France
and England) and carved glass (imported from Germany and
Bohemia), virtually destroyed engraved glass as an indigenous
art. It was resurrected in the inter-war period largely as the result
of the efforts of Helen Turner. Originally trained as a book
illustrator, she turned to the two-dimensional possibilities of
engraved glass in the 1930s and, having been awarded an Andrew
Grant fellowship, studied continental techniques, particularly
under Wilhelm von Eiff, Professor of Cutting and Engraving at
the Stuttgart School of Art and the leading exponent at that time
of the art of *Tiefschnitt* (deep-cutting). On her return to Scotland
at the beginning of the Second World War, Mrs Turner headed
the newly formed Glass Department in Edinburgh and for three
decades exerted an enormous influence on the development of
glass-engraving.

Since her retirement from teaching in 1972 she has worked
full-time at her studio in Juniper Green, south of Edinburgh and
has demonstrated her versatility in a wide range of techniques
from copper-wheel engraving on small articles such as goblets, to
sand-blasting and deep-cutting used in the production of large
bas-relief panels in glass. She was succeeded as Head of the Glass
Department by John Lawrie, her star pupil and long-time
collaborator both at the College and Juniper Studio. Their styles
are vastly different. Mrs Turner's style has been described by John
Lucas of the Design Council Scottish Committee as 'cool,
controlled, precise, superb', and to this one might add that in her
detailed treatment of landscape or rendering of natural motifs her
engraving has not been surpassed for its realism and subtle tonal
qualities. John Lawrie, on the other hand, epitomizes the new

generation of artists in this field. As Lucas has succinctly described him, he is 'experimental, exciting, wild at times, but great in his architectural concepts'.

Under the guidance and inspiration of Helen Turner and John Lawrie it is hardly surprising that much of the finest engraved glass produced today hails from Edinburgh, and the intricate copper-wheel engraving by Alison Geissler and Alison Kinnaird is therefore beyond the scope of this book. Harold Gordon of Greywalls Studio in Forres specializes in the engraving of vases, bowls, decanters and whisky glasses. Ann Bain of Balerno, Midlothian, uses copper-wheel engraving on lead crystal, while Helen Grainge of Garve in Wester Ross concentrates mainly on bird and animal subjects hand-engraved on hollow ware. Bruce Walker of Dyce, Aberdeenshire, engraves wildlife, scenery and portraiture on glass. Most of the craftsmen working on the decoration of glass utilize hollow ware produced by one or other of the more commercial glass-houses, and it is not uncommon for glass manufactured in England, Germany or Scandinavia to be employed for this purpose. Conversely, copper- and stone-wheel engraving, acid-etching and sand-blasting are techniques used by Strathearn and Caithness Glass in their more ornamental wares. Strathearn Glass have diversified from their original paperweights and now produce a wide range of decorative domestic glassware in clear and coloured glass. They have also recently begun to develop glass-engraving techniques.

Caithness Glass are justifiably renowned for their engraved glass, making use of the skills of such artists as Colin Terris and Denis Mann, both of whom are acknowledged as master-engravers in their own right. Deep-cutting and engraving on glass both transforms the basic article and adds a new dimension to the art of the engraver or carver, the special qualities of translucence enhancing the sculptural character of the work.

STAINED GLASS

Unlike most countries of western Europe Scotland has little in the way of an ancient tradition of stained glass. In the Middle Ages the religious houses and churches of Scotland would, like their European counterparts, have had stained glass windows, but the comparative poverty of the country at that date precluded the widespread usage of such luxuries. One of the less fortunate aspects of the Scottish Reformation in the sixteenth century was the destruction of stained glass windows as an outward sign of popery and the long taboo on this form of ecclesiastical adornment which subsequently came into force. This phobia was only gradually relaxed and the majority of the extant windows in Scottish churches belongs to the nineteenth century when glass painting was widely used as a relatively inexpensive substitute. It has to be admitted that much of the stained glass of that period was second-rate and it is regrettable that there are all too few opportunities at the present time for the development of an indigenous craft in stained glass. Church-building is not exactly a growth industry: the cost of maintaining existing churches is escalating rapidly and there are very few wealthy patrons willing to commission individual windows. Outside of Glasgow and Edinburgh there are few craftsmen of note at work in this medium. George Garson of East Burnside, West Lothian, works on commissioned windows and stained glass mural panels, but also produces smaller items such as glass mosaics and decorative panels suitable for house interiors. John Blyth, with more than forty years experience of this craft, has recently established a stained glass studio at Balbirnie.

The most prominent craftsman in stained glass today is Douglas Hogg of Kelso who established his studio there in 1971 and has since produced several important public commissions including the set of two windows in Thornton Parish Church near Kirkcaldy. Important commissions of this sort are expensive and time-consuming and understandably infrequent. He has subsequently diversified from leaded glass into resin-bonded glass murals and sculpture, using acrylic resins and various metals. Stained glass or its modern counterpart depends largely on transmitted light for full effect. For this reason it is an ideal medium for illuminated panels and lampshades. One has only to consider the present market value of the wisteria stained glass lampshades made by Tiffany in the early 1900s to appreciate the potential of modern glass mosaic shades. Here again is a craft which promises to become more important in years to come, as the demand for traditional stained glass windows on a large scale inevitably diminishes.

GLASS PAPERWEIGHTS

The superb millefiori confections of the leading French glass-houses – Baccarat, Clichy and St Louis – inspired paperweight production in other European countries, and even in the United States, in the second half of the nineteenth century. Millefiori

(Italian for a thousand flowers) is a form of decoration consisting of small sections of glass canes bedded in a base and covered by a clear glass dome. The range of stars, crimps and cogwheels in different colours is infinite and several hundred tiny pieces might be involved in a single paperweight in a patterned, scrambled or carpet ground. The millefiori technique of glass mosaic was known to the Egyptians and Romans but was revived by the Venetians and first used in glass paperweights in the early nineteenth century, whence it spread to Bohemia, Silesia and France and subsequently to England and the Untied States. Paperweights were made in the French manner in London and the West Midlands, while bottle-glass 'dumpies' were a speciality of the Yorkshire glass-houses, but there is little evidence of paperweights having been widely manufactured in Scotland. It is now thought that bottle-glass weights of the doorstop variety were made in the Portobello district of Midlothian, while John Ford of Edinburgh made weights encapsulating sulphide profiles of Robert Burns and other Scottish celebrities. Giant marbles, with opaque and coloured glass swirls and striations, were popular in Scotland in the nineteenth century, but whether they were all imported from England (Sunderland, in particular, being noted for them) or whether some were manufactured in Scotland is not known for certain. If the latter was the case, it seems surprising that these techniques were never applied to paperweights.

Paradoxically, though Scotland had little tradition of paperweight-making in the nineteenth century, it is in Scotland that the best British paperweights have been produced in the present century. Today there is only one firm in England making high quality millefiori weights compared with four in Scotland. The phenomenon of modern Scottish paperweights is largely the result of the efforts of one man, Paul Ysart, who has been active in this field for more than half a century and continues to produce fine paperweights which are eagerly prized by discerning collectors all over the world.

Ysart was born in Barcelona in 1904 of Bohemian parentage. With his family he moved to France shortly before the First World War and there his father Salvadore learned the techniques of glass-blowing, possibly at the St Louis glassworks. This is no more than surmise, though a miniature St Louis weight has been recorded in the style favoured by the early Ysart weights. In 1915 Salvadore Ysart and his family moved to Scotland and there he found employment at the Leith Flint Glassworks which then specialized in scientific and industrial glassware. His son Paul subsequently joined him and for a time worked on scientific glass before turning, in the early 1920s, to paperweights in traditional millefiori patterns. These early Ysart weights were strongly influenced by the mid-nineteenth century French weights, both in style and decoration and in the types of canes employed. These weights comprised concentric, spaced, garland or patterned millefiori motifs on a wide range of grounds, either translucent in shades of deep blue, green, red or purple, or mottled and opaque in tints ranging from pale pink to sandy yellow and flaming orange. A distinctive Ysart touch was the use of lengths of filigree cane sunk into the ground. Most of these weights incorporated a cane initialled 'PY'.

Ysart also made a number of flower and insect weights, always in a rather flat, two-dimensional style, and the most highly prized of these are his butterfly and dragonfly weights in coloured glass with a millefiori surround. Unlike the traditional French insect weights, Ysart's versions often used millefiori canes to make the wings and bodies, and this is a style which he has continued to employ down to the present day.

For the greater part of his career Paul Ysart worked in Perthshire but in the 1960s he moved north to Caithness and settled in Wick where he has a studio. At first he was associated with the Caithness Glass Company and to this period belong the paperweights containing the 'PY' cane and also the word 'Caithness' inscribed on their bases. Although he now works quite independently of Caithness Glass it is no coincidence that millefiori glass, ranging from paperweights to jewellery, is an important part of the company's output.

Other members of the Ysart family worked with Jim Moncrieff for many years at a small glassworks in Perth and evolved a distinctive type of glassware known as Monart. Eventually the family decided to form its own small factory in Perth and this traded as Ysart Brothers and latterly as the Vasart Glass Company. It continued to make vases, dishes and bowls in the Monart tradition, but also produced glass paperweights and related millefiori articles such as door knobs, glass-handled corkscrews and other bar novelties and cocktail equipment. It was this speciality that brought Vasart into contact with the whisky distillers, William Teacher and Sons, in 1963. Teachers were looking for a publicity gimmick and came up with the idea of one of their whisky bottles, complete with cap and label, but squashed flat to form a dish. The idea seemed so simple, but in practice it was difficult to translate into an article which could be easily produced. Eventually they passed the problem to Vasart and having surmounted the production difficulties, they were awarded the contract.

During their negotiations with Vasart and various visits to Perth to watch the progress of this project, executives of Teachers became fascinated with the craft of glass-blowing. At the same time they realized that if this enterprising glassworks was to survive in the competitive atmosphere of the modern glass industry it would require financial support. It seemed natural that a company engaged in one traditional Scottish industry should support another, and out of this mututal co-operation grew the Strathearn Glass Company, in which Teachers became the majority shareholders. The Strathearn glassworks moved to Crieff and production began at the end of 1964. At first Strathearn Glass continued to make glassware in the Vasart tradition and millefiori paperweights and related bibelots remain the most important part of their output to this day. These weights range in size from miniatures to magnums and include scrambled, concentric, carpet and patterned millefiori, spaced millefiori on a muslin ground, overlays, butterfly and flower weights. These weights are produced in unlimited editions though such is the nature of the craft that each paperweight is bound to be slightly different from all the others. Some of these unlimited weights incorporate an initial 'S' cane. At the same time Strathearn produce limited editions of crown and overlow weights, incorporating the initial 'S' cane and with the year of manufacture inscribed on the base. In recent years they have expanded their range beyond the traditional millefiori styles and have evolved distinctive Scottish paperweights, such as upright floral and faceted weights, and weights enclosing Scottish sand and ground gravel ('Stoer') or Scottish quartz encapsulated in clear colourless glass ('Ice Pool').

Four years after Strathearn Glass began operations at Crieff, Stuart Drysdale, a former director of Vasart, broke away from the new company to form his own glass-house. Drysdale took with him some of the best of the former Vasart craftsmen who wished to continue making traditional millefiori weights. Perthshire Paperweights, as their name implies, have since concentrated entirely on this medium. While Strathearn have diversified into other fields and have widened their paperweight techniques, Perthshire Paperweights have continued to produce millefiori weights of the very highest quality. As a result Perthshire Paperweights today enjoy a fine reputation for the highest standards of technique and finish and their limited editions are universally regarded as among the finest paperweights anywhere in the world. The brilliant range of colours and designs in the millefiori canes, matched by the flawless perfection of the surrounding clear glass globes, is the equal of anything produced by the great French glass-houses at the height of their paperweight careers.

Much of the success of Perthshire Paperweights is due to Jack Allan and Anton Moravec who produce the more sumptuous paperweights, including faceted overlay weights and subject weights featuring dragonflies and other insects. These weights are engraved on the base with the date and the initials 'JA' and 'AM' and are sold with a numbered certificate. A more recent development consists of special Christmas weights. There is also a wide selection of millefiori and insect weights in the cheaper, unlimited range. Some Perthshire weights incorporate an initial 'P' cane, while a characteristic feature of many of their weights is a dead flat base with a star-cut ornament in the centre.

In 1971 Caithness Glass began producing its own distinctive paperweights, breaking away from the Ysart millefiori tradition. Although these weights have the characteristic paperweight profile, with a raised dome and flat base, the motifs were unlike anything produced before, exploiting the qualities of the glass itself without recourse to multicoloured canes and using air bubbles to create an illusion of silvery spheres in suspension. Paperweights were produced in unlimited and limited editions, the latter bearing the initials of the craftsman and the date on the base. The paperweights produced in 1972 had a suitably lunar motif, alluding to the recent Apollo moon-landings. 'Starbase' had an abstract design sumbolizing a space station of the future spinning in outer space, with the planet Earth below. 'Orbit' is an abstract interpretation of the unknown we may one day discover in the exploration of outer space, with a silvery ring representing a space vehicle in orbit above the surface of some unknown planet. Viewing these fascinating weights from different angles, and letting the light fall on the strange moonscape and spatial atmosphere, we are looking at something magic – scarcely anything so mundane as glass. In the shape of the Caithness paperweights of the 1970s we can see the shape of things to come – a far cry from the close millefiori of Baccarat or Clichy.

Caithness craftsmen and designers, Peter Holmes and Colin Terris, are continuing to experiment with new forms and techniques. Among the paperweights being produced in 1974 were globes whose coruscated interiors were festooned with tiny silvery bubbles creating a frosted effect. Another recent innovation has been the use of deep cutting as external ornament to the top of the globe, in stars and ice-crystal patterns.

John Airlie began producing paperweights in 1972, using the pale blue and dark green glass associated with his vases and other decorative wares. Airlie's Kirkhill paperweights are lower and flatter than the Caithness profile and rely entirely on random patterns of bubbles for ornament. More recently Peter Layton has added paperweights to his repertoire at Morar. By contrast, his weights have a relatively high, narrow profile, somewhat smaller than the doorstop 'dumpies' which Kilner produced in Wakefield over a century ago. There the resemblance ends, for Layton's paperweights consist of a high dome of clear colourless glass over a sphere of coloured glass in rich greens and blues, speckled with brown metallic oxide tears and clear silvery bubbles.

Apart from paperweights, Perthshire Paperweights and Strathearn Glass produce a wide range of related millefiori novelties, such as ash-trays, sweet-meat dishes, ink-pots, scent bottles and small decanters with millefiori decoration in the stoppers and bases. Caithness Glass use millefiori canes extensively in jewellery, such as rings, ear-rings and cuff-links.

SYNTHETIC GLASS

Since the Second World War various plastics have taken the place of glass in domestic and industrial use and it was inevitable that these substances should also have attracted the attention of the craftworker. Of the many types of plastics, acrylic and polyester resin are those which have found the widest application to craftwork. The craft applications of acrylic have already been touched upon, in the chapter on floral art, but this material is also used extensively in decorative panels and small sculpture. Most of this work is produced at present in the art colleges and has not as yet graduated to the status of a craft practised on a commercial scale.

Shattered polyester is used by Shattaline of Evanton in Ross-shire in the manufacture of lamp-bases, vases, book-ends, desk accessories and paperweights. The crushed and fragmented appearance of the plastic within the body of the object catches the light at different angles and produces an unusual lustrous effect. The same company also use fibreglass extensively in the production of decorative items. Liquid polyester resins are now widely used in the classroom to teach children the rudiments of cold-casting. Any natural object – dried flowers and plants, seashells, pebbles, pieces of wood, insects, crabs, butterflies and dried seeds – may be encapsulated in resin providing it is dried and preserved first, and as inexpensive kits and materials are now available this has become a very popular pastime. Very little art or craft is actually required to produce jewellery, key-rings, fobs and pendants encapsulating natural objects, but more skill is required to produce larger objects, such as plaques and paperweights enclosing a montage of natural objects. Fynecraft of Otter Ferry, for example, specialize in acrylic or polyester resin paperweights featuring crabs, shells and other specimens of marine life. Acrylic paperweights are also produced by the Harris Craft Guild, who utilize natural materials available in the Outer Hebrides, and by Martyn and Elaine King of Sanday (Orkney) and the craft workshop at John o' Groats.

Round-and square- top Orkney chairs, constructed and woven in their homes by craftsmen on the island of Westray.

Drawing out molten glass to form the canes for millefiori paperweights.

Copper-wheel engraving on glass.

(*opposite*) Cutting antler tines to produce staghorn buttons and jewellery.

Much knitwear is now produced on small machines, although the patterned yokes are still hand-knitted.

The intricate patterns used in sweaters, tam o'shanters and cushion covers vary from island to island. A group of knitters on Westray.

Saddlery and leatherwork from Beauly, Inverness-shire.

A clarsach or Scottish harp, being constructed by Ian Firth of St Andrews.

Two stages in making bag-pipes: (*above*) a block of African black wood being cut; (*below*) assembling the finished components.

David Illingworth of the Far North Pottery, Balnakeil.

Robert Park of the Culloden Pottery, Gollanfield.

Functional and decorative pottery produced at Munlochy, Ross and Cromarty.

[10]
Hornwork

Traditionally horn provided the Scots with the raw material for many useful articles as well as decorative wares. In the sixteenth to eighteenth centuries cow horn was widely used in the manufacture of spoons of different sizes and shapes and considerable ingenuity was shown in the application of this somewhat unpromising material to larger articles, such as quaichs and cups. This required the horn to be boiled until it was pliable and could be cut along one side, opened out and flattened under pressure and heat. Horn and bone were carved or incised and incorporated into the lids and side panels of caskets. Cow horns were more readily adapted for use as powder flasks, the narrow point mounted with a brass or pewter stopper and the wider end plugged by a wooden or leather disc. The flattened sides of these powder horns were frequently embellished with carving and pokerwork, using the non-figurative tracery and Celtic scrollwork for which the west of Scotland and Ireland have long been famous. Relatively few examples of horns decorated with skrimshaw pictures have survived and this seems to suggest that such highly intricate pictorial decoration was not favoured as much as the Celtic tracery. The advent of cheap leather and metal powder flasks in the eighteenth century killed this ancient art. At the same time metal flatware and pottery superseded horn spoons and bowls and hornwork thus joined the other crafts which had been allowed to die out.

Ramshorn, however, was used extensively in the Lowlands and Southern Uplands where sheep-farming was well-established in the seventeenth and eighteenth centuries. Ramshorn lacks the smooth, comparatively large surface of cowhorn and is therefore not so suitable for decorative treatment, or for adaptation to flat or oval surfaces as in snuff-boxes and other small boxes. On the other hand, its gnarled, craggy appearance intrigued craftsmen, who turned these qualities to good advantage and produced small decorative articles such as snuff-mulls, which resembled miniature powder flasks and were generally mounted in silver. In the nineteenth century these ramshorn mulls enjoyed a certain vogue and to this period belong the examples which were richly carved and mounted, often incorporating a cairngorm or some other semi-precious stone set in the lid.

The chief use to which ramshorn was put, however, was the manufacture of the decorative heads of shepherds' crooks and walking sticks. Crooks, cromachs and cleeks were widely produced all over the sheep-farming areas of the south and over the last three hundred years various regional and district styles have emerged. The making of shepherds crooks is widely practised to this day and though it spread to the Highlands in the wake of the sheep invasion of the late eighteenth and nineteenth centuries (associated with the Highland Clearances), it is still largely a Lowland art, judging by the predominantly Border origin of the prize-winners at the Royal Highland Show each year, where the various sections devoted to crooks and walking sticks always attract keen competition. This is a craft which is practised by shepherds themselves and is one of the very few genuinely rural crafts which have continued without interruption down to the present time.

The Cheviot sheep fared little better in the Highlands than the people it displaced and by the mid-nineteenth century the sheepruns were giving way to the vast deer forests established for the sport of southern gentlemen. The deer which roam the Highland hills and moors have provided the local craftsman with the third material in this group – staghorn. If anything, this is an even more intractable material than ramshorn at first glance, but though the branching antlers of the Highland stag are unsuitable for larger articles, its craggy exterior, contrasting with the ivory quality of the interior, make it an ideal substance for small decorative items, such as buttons, brooches, cuff-links and other forms of jewellery. The tines or points of the antlers, when reasonably straight, are ideal for the shafts of Highland cutlery and the handles of ornamental dirks worn with Highland dress.

All three types of horn are used by James Young of Comrie in the production of useful and decorative articles. Elsewhere in Scotland craftsmen tend to specialize in one or other varieties of horn. Staghorn is perhaps the material most often found in the Highland area in the form of jewellery, cutlery and table decorations, and it is even incorporated in the bases of lamps. In this field the most prominent craftsmen are Cameron Thomson of Aberfeldy (who also produces cowhorn articles), Glenroy

Horncraft of Braemar and White Mountain Crafts of Grantown-on-Spey. Curiously enough, several craftsmen working in the Lowlands also specialize in staghorn products. Staghorn articles of very high quality and in a wide variety of designs are made by Air Commodore Carill-Worsley of Moniaive in Dumfriesshire. John Forsyth of Alva, Clackmannanshire, produces jewellery and that distinctive form of Highland dagger known as a *sgian dubh* (literally 'black knife') decorated with staghorn.

Not surprisingly, Ayrshire, in the heart of the dairy-farming country, is the chief venue for cowhorn products, which include ornamental shoe-lifts, fish lamps and table lamps, hunting horns, ship models with horn hulls and sails, tableware such as vases and cruet sets, and above all the full range of spoons from diminutive egg and salt spoons to salad servers. The principal groups of craftsmen involved are St Inan Products of Dalmellington and Horncraft Ltd of Irvine. Hornwork jewellery and small decorative items are widely produced all over the Highland area and are to be found in craft shops from Argyll to Caithness. Probably the best places to find the general range of horncraft are the Horn Shop in Braemar, the Old Post Office in Pitlochry and Earra Gael at Tarbert, but excellent hornware is also produced by the Garve Work Society in Wester Ross and Kyleside Weaving and Handcraft at Bonar Bridge in Sutherland. William Duncan of Kelton in Kircudbrightshire makes a wide range of hornware articles, from cutlery and jewellery to flower vases. Grant McPherson of Caledonian Hardwoods in Renfrewshire uses staghorn inlay on various hardwoods for table lamps and ornaments, while Heathergems of East Kilbride make heather mosiac jewellery inset in staghorn.

[11]

Jewellery

Scottish jewellery is exceedingly versatile in the materials and techniques it makes use of and every aspect is covered in this chapter. Allied crafts, such as lapidary work and silversmithing, are dealt with in separate chapters, though their application to jewellery is discussed here.

Historically, Scottish jewellery tended towards the functional rather than the purely decorative; for this reason the bulk of the antique pieces consist of brooches and buckles and there is little emphasis on rings, pendants, bracelets or necklaces prior to the mid-nineteenth century. Much of the jewellery worn by the upper class in the earlier period was imported from France or the Low Countries. Thereafter the more ornamental jewellery of the upper classes, in gold, silver and precious stones, continued to reflect English or continental fashions, whereas the more functional jewellery of the lower classes continued in the Celtic tradition. Though silver was widely used, other metals, such as pewter, copper, brass and even iron, were often employed, while semi-precious stones and polished pebbles took the place of gemstones. Whereas the jewels worn by the nobility were fashioned by foreign craftsmen working mainly in the Edinburgh area, or were imported from other countries, the jewellery of the lower classes was largely produced by itinerant craftsmen known as *ceards*. These tinkers enjoyed a nomadic existence, going from door to door and district to district plying their trade. Traditional patterns were handed on from one generation of *ceards* to the next and styles in buckles and brooches remained virtually unchanged for centuries.

These traditional forms were 'discovered' and taken up by commercial jewellers in the mid-nineteenth century when Celtic romanticism was all the rage. Much of this commercial jewellery, with glass-paste cairngorms set in silver-plated mountains with over-elaborate tracery and a riot of thistles, was not produced in Scotland at all, but emanated from Dublin, Birmingham and even Germany. These pieces were eclectic in style, drawing freely on Celtic, Norse and Anglo-Saxon motifs. This taste in jewellery reflected current fashions in literature – the novels of Sir Walter Scott, the Arthurian legends popularized by Tennyson and the Icelandic sagas translated by William Morris. It bore little resemblance, of course, to the true jewellery of people which continued to be fashioned by the Highland tinkers. Inevitably, however, people spurned the authentic article for the bastard imitation and though a few *ceards* were still making traditional plaid brooches as late as the 1930s theirs was a dying craft.

In the 1890s Frances and Margaret MacDonald led the so-called Glasgow school of designers who rejected the Balmoralization of Scottish jewellery and attempted to get back to first principles. Their jewellery is often described as Art Nouveau but that is utterly misleading since their style was more angular and rectilinear and inspired not so much by plant motifs (as were the French and Belgian designers) as by the human figure. Their figures were elongated to the point of absurdity, and their jewellery and metalwork designs were often derided by their contemporaries who referred to them as the 'spook school'. The MacDonald sisters abandoned jewellery after about 1910 but their lasting legacy to the generation of craftworkers who came after them was their use of base metals, principally copper and pewter, inlaid with enamels, fused glass and semi-precious stones. Indirectly, the activities of the MacDonald sisters, Herbert McNair and Talwin Morris initiated the revival of jewellery as a craft in the 1920s. This revival was not so uncompromising in its rejection of nineteenth-century styles, techniques and materials but was nevertheless a refreshing change from the stereotyped neo-Celtic jewellery which was still being mass-produced at that time.

The revival of fine quality, hand-made jewellery in the inter-war period is epitomized in the work of Norah Creswick who, now in her nineties, remains in the forefront of the craft to this day. Mrs Creswick was born in Birmingham where, ironically, much of the more atrocious Celtic jewellery of the nineteenth and early twentieth centuries was produced. She trained as a musician and only turned to jewellery some years later, encouraged by her husband who was a practising silversmith and a lecturer in metalwork at the Edinburgh College of Art. Her jewellery is in the best tradition of the Arts and Crafts movement of the late nineteenth century which rejected the spurious and

returned to natural forms. Her best-known work consists of the
Clan Sprays – jewellery incorporating the plant and flower
symbols of the Scottish clans – and her bee rings, combining gold
and silver with stones such as turquoise, amethyst and tourmaline
in honey-bee motifs. Since the Second World War, a new
generation of craftsmen have turned to jewellery, and the current
range is astonishingly varied both in materials and style.

BROOCHES

The form of jewellery associated with Scotland above all others
is the brooch, which assumed a special importance as a dress
accessory for both sexes at a very early date and continued to be
the chief item of jewellery until the beginning of the present
century. This was largely due to the peculiar nature of Scottish
clothing, with the accent on loosefitting garments and plaids
which were held in place by pins and fastenings out of which the
distinctive forms of Scottish brooch evolved. In its most primitive
form the brooch consisted of a piece of bone, and rudimentary
fasteners of this type actually survived in many parts of the
Highlands and Islands until the late nineteenth century. In more
sophisticated society, however, bone and wood fasteners were
superseded by metal brooches of a simple, pennanular type
common to the Bronze Age peoples of northern Europe.
Copper, silver and even gold were worked into brooches, and
intricate Celtic wire decoration applied to the pin and the clasps.
In the more elaborate forms developed in the Middle Ages native
pearls and semi-precious stones were mounted on brooches.
Hammered, chased and occasionally cast ornament in animal,
plant or human form were added. Later techniques such as *champlevé* enamelling and niello work were applied to the flat surfaces.

   Brooches varied enormously in size and some of the plaid
brooches of the eighteenth century were up to seven inches in
diameter, though three to four inches was about average. The
early eighteenth century was the heyday of the Highland plaid
brooch, with different styles adapted to the various garments
they secured. Thus one may distinguish between the large plaid
brooches, the simpler shawl brooches and the elongated kilt pins.
After the proscription of Highland dress as a result of the Jacobite
Rebellion of 1745-6, the production of these distinctive brooches
went into decline. The relaxation of the ban on Highland dress
came too late for its restoration as the every-day garb of the
Highlander, but Lowland enthusiasm for Highland dress,

inspired by the example of none other than Queen Victoria herself, led to a great expansion in the popularity of Scottish brooches and the development of many new designs. To the second half of the nineteenth century belong the highly ornate brooches in octagonal or circular disc form, those comprising concentric circles lavishly adorned with thistles, stags' heads and similar motifs and the silver brooches incorporating clan crests and other emblems.

This revival of the brooch coincided with the exploration of new materials. Semi-precious stones became fashionable in the late nineteenth century and have remained popular to this day. Cairngorms were a particular favourite as the focal point of plaid brooches and kilt pins, but for the first time attention was also paid to the wealth of hardstones, such as serpentine, agate and jasper which were polished and arranged in the settings of brooches using the *zellenmosaik* technique developed by Saxon jewellers in the late eighteenth century. Pebble brooches went out of fashion at the turn of the century but have been revived with conspicuous success in recent years. Other materials were utilized in the brooches produced in the late nineteenth century, mainly for sale to the late-Victorian and Edwardian tourists who began flocking to the Highlands each summer. These took the form of plume and claw brooches in which the fastening element was subordinate to the purely decorative aspects of natural materials. Plumecraft developed out of the traditional Highland practice of fashioning the badges of chiefs and chieftains from the feathers of eagle and blackcock, but it probably owed something to the influence of nineteenth-century fashion which popularized the use of feathers in hair ornaments and costume accessories. Less easy to understand, perhaps, was the late-Victorian penchant for brooches made of the feet of predatory birds. There were talismanic overtones about these 'claw' brooches – analogous to the lucky rabbit's foot charms which survive to this day. The feet of the ptarmigan were particularly prized for this purpose but in more recent years the feet of its humbler cousin, the Scottish red grouse, provide a satisfactory alternative. Plume and claw brooches are invariably combined with cairngorms. The resulting confection may well be redolent of the grouse moors and the lofty Cairngorms, but its Scottishness is rather artificial and bears little resemblance to the simple brass or silver brooches and pins worn by the Highlander in days gone by. Plume and claw brooches, however, are among the most popular items produced by the craft jewellers today and because they are imbued with a quintessential Scottish flavour they will doubtless continue to be one of the best-selling lines in the tourist market. It would be impossible to name all the jewellers involved in this lucrative trade, but the more prominent ones include Garvie of Kilmore (near Oban), Highland Craft Producers of Beauly, Kilmartin Crafts, Ness Agencies of Inverness, Schimacraft of Glenelg, Russcraft of Aviemore, Aileen Wilson of Bunchrew and Wilson Scottish Crafts of Inverness.

It must not be imagined that brooches were entirely the prerogative of the Highlander, and at least one major type of Lowland brooch has survived to this day. Luckenbooth brooches take their name from the Luckenbooths, the wooden stalls near St Giles' Cathedral in Edinburgh, where brooches and favours were made and sold in the seventeenth and eighteenth centuries. These brooches were made of silver and sometimes gold and were heart-shaped. Occasionally they consisted of two hearts entwined and the more elaborate examples were set with semi-precious stones. Other variants feature twin sets of initials and dates. These brooches were designed as love tokens and were extremely popular up to the early nineteenth century. They have since been revived and are now a standard feature of the repertoire of the craftsmen working in silver all over Scotland and are no longer confined to the Edinburgh area. Fortunately, new life has been given to the Luckenbooth brooches by jewellers in different parts of the country who have tried as far as possible to formulate their own variants in shape, styling, engraving, enamelling, inlay and the use of pebbles and semi-precious stones.

OTHER FORMS OF JEWELLERY
Although brooches are the mainstay of the craft jewellery produced today they are by no means the only article being made. Other pieces of jewellery include rings, earrings, cuff-links, pendants, necklaces and bracelets but, like the brooches, they tend to be tourist-orientated. Much of the current output has been criticized for merely restating the Celtic forms of design without truly rekindling the Celtic spirit. On the other hand, it would be quite unfair to suggest that Scottish craft jewellery is a debased object of tourist sentiment. The craftsman (who must also be a businessman) knows what will sell well and may be forgiven for concentrating on familiar lines and

traditional motifs which have stood the test of time. Since jewellery is probably the most popular of all tourist souvenirs on account of its compactness, it is hardly surprising that most craftsmen tend not to be very adventurous in exploring new forms or media. Moreover, within the context of traditional Celtic and Nordic design it is quite heartening to observe what a vast range of motifs have been produced in present-day craft jewellery. In many instances artists have been inspired by local relics of the past, such as carved stone crosses, bosses and roundels. This type of ornament, derived from sculpture and architecture, is to be found in the silver jewellery produced all over Scotland, from Fife to Cromarty, from Galloway to Inverness. It is particularly true of the jewellery currently produced in Orkney and Shetland by Ola Gorie and Ortak of Kirkwall and J.G. Rae of Shetland Silvercraft for example. Local and regional motifs, often of great antiquity, are also to be found in the jewellery using modern techniques – enamelled copper and pewer, nail sculpture and wrought iron and even ceramic jewellery. While most of the 'traditional' jewellery is derived from Celtic, Norse or medieval motifs, John Prince of Creetown in Galloway has gone even farther back in time for inspiration, modelling his bronze and silver pendants and love tokens on Greek and Roman trinkets excavated from sites around the Roman Wall.

There has been little attempt so far to explore the potential of materials not traditionally associated with jewellery. The application of staghorn to this medium, discussed in the previous chapter, is an exception and allied to this has been the fairly recent application of vegetable material to jewellery. The best example is provided by Heathergems of East Kilbride who have exploited the characteristics of heather stems and roots, their asymmetrical form in section and delicate figuring, and have transformed this unlikely material into pendants and brooches. By dyeing the stems in various colours before drying them, greater variety can be achieved. The stems are banded together in various patterns and sawn into thin mosaic sections, adapting a technique used two centuries ago by the makers of Tunbridge woodware. The resulting marquetry veneers in miniature are mounted on a staghorn base, varnished and polished.

Hardwoods as a medium for jewellery are beginning to attract the serious attention of craftsmen. Brooches and pendants composed of hardwood chips decorated with pokerwork and carving are currently being produced by several craftsmen, notably Ian Strachan of Aboyne and J.K. Scott Lodge of Cromarty. Decorated slipware pottery is a popular medium for jewellery, principally pendants and earrings, and this is a sideline of craft pottery which is growing in importance. The application of millefiori glass to jewellery by Caithness Glass is discussed in Chapter 10.

At the other end of the scale there is a small but highly important group of craftsmen working entirely in silver, gold and semi-precious stones whose work transcends the 'bread and butter' jewellery of the tourist trade. The jewels fashioned by Norman Cherry of Kelso, Kenneth Derby of Cromarty, R.A.M. Dickson of Tayport, Norman Grant of Lundin Links, William and Lilian Hall of Rothesay and Janet Stollery of Cullen belong to the realm of fine art rather than the crafts. It is to artists of their calibre that one must look for the refreshing, the exciting and the original in Scottish jewellery today. Because of the intrinsic value of the materials the jewellery produced by these craftsmen seldom percolates down to the craft shops on the tourist beat. Much of their work consists of individually commissioned pieces or finds its way immediately to the more select jewellery shops of Edinburgh, Glasgow and London, while a not inconsiderable volume of their work is exported to the Untied States and Canada.

[12]
Knitwear, Crochet and Macramé

In times gone by the isolation of many communities forced them to rely heavily on clothing which they could produce themselves. The ready availability of wool ensured that knitting was a skill practised by young and old and by men and women alike. Gradually what had begun as a necessity developed into a craft and, in certain parts of the country, eventually became an art which is recognized as such all over the world today. Scottish knitwear now ranks with whisky and tweeds among the country's top exports. The development of tourism, however, has been something of a mixed blessing in that it stimulated greater demand for Scottish knitwear than the knitters could produce. Since the Second World War a mechanical element has crept in and much of the cottage knitwear of the present day is worked on a knitting machine, though it is still necessary to finish the garments by hand. The more intricate patterns, of course, have to be knitted by hand, but here again the demands of the market have forced many knitters to give up all-over patterned knitwear and concentrate on machine-knitted bodies with hand-knitted yokes. The economics of hand-knitting have created this situation. Hand-knitters producing beautiful jerseys with all-over patterns were never recompensed properly for the labour and skill involved. It is only now that the public is beginning to wake up to the fact that if it wants fine examples of all-over hand-knitted articles it must pay an economic price for it. The situation was also exacerbated by the structure of the retail trade in hand-knitted goods. Ruairidh MacLeod, Secretary of the Harris Craft Guild, criticizing the mark-up on craft-made articles sold by retailers, cites the case of a first-class knitter who can produce one fine sweater per week, and receives £5.50 for a garment which involves fifty hours knitting – an average wage of elevenpence an hour. Yet the same sweater will sell in a retail shop for fifteen or sixteen pounds.

The elements of sweated labour and exploitation by the retailer are much more evident in knitwear than in any other Scottish craft for several reasons. Knitting is one of the few rural crafts which are genuinely so, being carried on by crofters in the Highlands and Islands to eke out the subsistence economy of fishing and farming. Knitting was largely an occupation of the long winter months when other activities were curtailed by the weather. In many cases knitting was introduced over a century ago as a means of relieving the poverty of the peasantry and the knitwear was purchased by charitable organizations (mainly in the Lowlands) for retail at church bazaars and sales of work. This created an atmosphere of do-goodery which lingers on to this day, though there is something ironical in the belief that retailers are doing craftworkers a favour by purchasing goods at low prices and marking them up steeply 'in case they don't sell'.

Admittedly the situation has changed dramatically in recent years and the organization of co-operative bodies and craft guilds in many parts of the Highlands has helped to reduce the gap between actual cost and mark-up, and guarantee a better rate of pay for the hand-knitter, but there is a fear that improvement in retail distribution may have come too late. Undoubtedly knitting as a craft will continue, and the extension of direct selling (which is now a common feature of other crafts) may actually lead to a revival of knitting as an art, with the emphasis on all-over patterned articles. It is a sad fact, however, that traditional hand-knitting in Orkney and Shetland is dying. Television, which relieves the tedium of the long northern winter, has been blamed for the curtailment of hand-knitting as a pastime, but the oil boom is a more decisive factor. The influx of people and money to Orkney and Shetland is producing a larger indigenous market for knitwear but as oil-related industries develop they are providing a much more lucrative alternative especially to the younger generation of islanders.

So long as the islanders themselves appreciate the skill and artistry involved in the all-over patterned garments they will continue to be made, but already there are signs that production is falling sharply. There will always be a few dedicated craftsmen who will continue to knit for their own pleasure, but the pressures of current economic developments in the far north appear to be having an adverse long-term effect on knitting as a cottage industry. This is counterbalanced to some extent by the spread of hand-knitting to other parts of the country not traditionally associated with the cottage industry. Though much of the knitwear produced in the Borders is semi-mechanized and often organized as an adjunct of the great woollen mills of that region, there are now several craft knitters from Berwickshire to Galloway engaged in the production of shawls, gloves, scarves, jerseys and tam o' shanters in distinctive patterns, sometimes even using hand-dyed and spun wool. Although the patterns now used in much of the hand knitwear are often a mixture of styles, even including Norwegian and Irish (especially Aran) styles, the home workers of the far north and the north-east still stick to traditional patterns.

FAIR ISLE

It is quite remarkable that Fair Isle, one of the most remote and sparsely populated islands of Scotland, should have produced a form of knitting which is one of the most interesting examples of the art anywhere in Europe. Today, this highly distinctive form of multi-coloured knitting is widely practised not only in the northern islands but all over the Scottish mainland. True Fair Isle patterns are variations on a style known as the Armada Cross, which is Spanish in origin and not Scandinavian like the styles evolved in Orkney and Shetland. It is not known how these multicoloured patterns found their way to this isolated spot but a popular theory is that these motifs were taught to the islanders by Spaniards from one of the Armada ships wrecked on the island. A more plausible version is that the islanders copied these stitches from the clothing found on the corpses of Spanish seaman washed ashore in the aftermath of the Armada gales. Certainly this ornate form of knitting was well documented in the seventeenth century, so references to the ill-starred Armada of 1588 are probably not far short of the mark. Though there is still some multi-coloured knitting done on the island, · under the encouragement of the National Trust for Scotland who now own it, most of the so-called Fair Isle knitting is produced in other parts of Scotland, and, indeed, the term has come to be used for any kind of ornately patterned coloured knitting.

SHETLAND

Apart from the Fair Isle styles, the Shetlanders have their own characteristic knitting patterns which differ from the Fair Isle primarily in colouring and formation. True Shetland styles were noted for geometric motifs and the use of dark silhouettes – deep brown, grey or black – against lighter coloured wool. Originally Shetland patterns were executed in natural-coloured wool, the whites, creams and fawns contrasting with the darker shades found in Shetland sheep. The wool was simply scoured and spun without the addition of vegetable or mineral colouring of any kind. Nowadays, however, wool in a wide range of colours is employed to achieve the same results, but this multicoloured effect is relatively recent.

The most northerly of the Shetland islands, Unst, has long been noted for its lace-knitting used for christening robes, shawls and stoles. Though produced from wool the yarn is hand-spun into a soft, fine thread and the resulting lace is as delicate as gossamer. The patterns are as intricate as cobwebs and suggest a long history of development. Yet Unst lace knitting is a relatively modern phenomenon, roughly contemporary with the Ayrshire whitework mentioned in Chapter 5. The inspiration for this particular craft came from Europe early in the nineteenth century, and was introduced by Jessie Scanlon who had made a collection of Italian, French and Belgian lace while touring the Continent. She showed her collection of hand-made lace to the Hunter family of Unst and they were inspired to copy it. The ladies of the Hunter family adapted the Flemish and Venetian lace patterns to suit hand knitting and eventually produced their own distinctive styles. Christening shawls knitted by the Hunters were presented to Queen Victoria and successive generations of the British royal family have had christening shawls knitted by members of the same family until fairly recently. The last member of the Hunter family actually engaged on this delicate work died in the 1950s, but by that time the skills which she practised had been passed on to other women of Unst. Nevertheless it is a matter for some concern that few people are carrying on the tradition of lace-knitting and this unique craft is in danger of dying out entirely.

The patterns have never been properly written down and, in the true fashion of craftsmanship of centuries ago, they have been passed from mother to daughter by visual and oral tradition. Basically, the patterns are composed of a series of simple lace stitches formed into diamonds, hexagons and stripes. The counter-change of patterns has resulted in a wide variety of designs, so that no two examples of lace-knitting are ever identical. There are about a dozen major patterns, with names which are both picturesque and descriptive, such as 'Crest of the Wave', 'Feather and Fan', 'Fern', 'Madeira' and 'Ladder and Cat's Paw', and inevitably there is a 'Mrs Hunter's Pattern' which perpetuates the memory of the family which pioneered this art.

Knitwear from the Shetland home workers is collected and retailed through several companies, such as the Shetland Knitters' Association in Lerwick, the Reawick Lamb Marketing Company and Thuleknit (the lastnamed having an office in Edinburgh) but can also be obtained from T.M. Adie & Sons of Voe and Peter Johnson of Bixter.

FISHERMEN'S SWEATERS

Sealskin waistcoats and jackets were traditionally the favourite garments of fishermen in the northern islands and in the fishing ports dotted round the coasts of Caithness, Sutherland and the Moray Firth, but in the eighteenth century, as the seal population declined and wool became more common, the sweaters favoured by English fishermen became more popular in Scotland. The strong influence of the Channel Islands, where knitting was a well-established industry in the sixteenth century, can be seen in the Gaelic word for a fisherman's sweater – *gannsaidh* – derived from the bailiwick of Guernsey where these thick, dark-blue 'ganseys' originated. Traditional ganseys had a characteristically square shape and were knitted on five needles without a seam, the arms being knitted in. These garments were designed for hard wear in all weathers and were noted for their rugged appearance, thick cuffs and stout, stand-up collar secured by buttons. The knitting of ganseys was a labour of love and a great deal of pride went into the making of these elaborately patterned sweaters. Each district and fishing port had its own distinctive style, and each knitter devised her own variant, so that the range of patterns is almost infinite. Over the years the patterns on fishermen's sweaters evolved their own form of heraldry and symbolism. The four cables represented the pillars of the world, the zigzag patterns represented marriage lines, hearts and diamonds symbolized love and wealth, and the 'Ladder of Life' stitch possessed talismanic qualities. These elements were common to many of the patterns, but their arrangement was often peculiar to a particular locality. Experts can identify a sweater by its stitches and can assign it to a port between Lerwick in the north and St Monance in the south. Nowadays fishermen are forsaking the old patterned ganseys and showing a preference for plain styles, and already many of the old stitches have disappeared. The revival of interest in crafts generally has come just in time to prevent this art from dying out. Today the traditional dark blue ganseys vie with the cream-coloured Aran sweaters in popularity with the tourist trade though they are no longer confined to the north-east. Patterned fishermen's sweaters are available through the firms mentioned above, and also from such companies as Scalpay Knitwear of Harris, Viking of Beauly, Catherine of Inverness, Scotcrafts of Peterhead and Scotnord of Crieff.

OTHER STYLES
Jerseys, distinguished from ganseys by being thinner and generally more colourful, are also produced in the northern isles and the north-east mainland, but are extensively knitted all over the country in a wide variety of styles and patterns. In recent years the growth of winter sports in the Cairngorms has stimulated the development of knitted ski-wear and the patterns used in this context are derived from a wide range of European styles, from Icelandic and Norwegian to Tyrolean. These eclectic styles are a recent phenomenon and, as yet, account for only a small proportion of the patterns used. Traditional Scottish mainland patterns vary from modifications of the fishermen's styles (cable and seeded rib patterns) to checks and mock tartans. The latter consist either of a mock kilting in which wool of the same colour is used throughout to produce raised stitching simulating the lines and squares of tartan, or a combination of a ground shade with four or five contrasting colours in imitation of the clan tartans.

Chequer patterns are not always based on the Highland tartans (themselves a comparatively modern innovation), and many of the checks found in Border knitwear have a long history in themselves. The best known of the Lowland checks are those which originated in the Dumfriesshire town of Sanquhar, famous for its connection with the Covenanters. The Sanquhar, patterns used two sharply contrasting colours of wool – brown and 'natural' or dark grey and white. From these sober combinations were derived a multiplicity of chequer patterns knitted in small squares, the ornament consisting mainly of motifs picked out in the lighter wool against the darker squares. Sanquhar patterns spread all over the Southern Uplands from Galloway to Berwickshire and are used to this day in the knitting of gloves, mitts and stockings. This type of knitwear is produced by May Roberts of Lochmaben, Galloway Lodge Cottage Industries of Gatehouse of Fleet, and Mrs L. MacDonald of Cockburnspath.

CROCHET AND MACRAME

Crochet work became popular in Scotland in the mid-nineteenth century and rapidly won the enthusiasm of countless young ladies who, with more energy than genius, produced an enormous quantity of table mats, antimacassars and tidies, and adapted fine crochet to produce a kind of lace which was widely employed in the decoration of clothing. The simplicity and rapidity of the work, however, tended to militate against its acceptance as a serious craft. It continued to be taught to young girls at home and in school and was practised sporadically as a pastime with few pretensions to artistry or originality. Crochet work was given a new lease of life after the Second World War when its stitches and techniques were adapted to bolder and more colourful work and extended to a wide range of dramatic chunky objects, from belts, ties and girdles to wall hangings, waistcoats and even jewellery. This resurgence of interest in crochet and its adaptation to new forms has also been accompanied by the development of more distinctive patterns and stitches. As a result, the craft crochet of the present day offers visual excitement which bears little resemblance to the rather shapeless, lacy jumpers with which crochet was traditionally associated. Fine crochet work is still practised, of course. It may be found in shawls and stoles, and it continues to form the basis for the production of textile mats and covers, but here again new life has been injected into these media, reflecting the rejection of hackneyed forms and the quest for new and original designs which characterize the modern craft scene in general.

Most of the crochet work available to the public is produced by home workers whose output is handled by a number of larger organizations such as Tweedbits of Galashiels, the Harris Craft Guild and the Isle of Sanday Knitters Company of Orkney. In most cases crochet work is only incidental to the main product of knitwear or hand-woven tweeds but Handmaids (whose registered office is actually in London) concentrates mainly on crocheted articles. P.A.T.'s of King Duncan's Road, Inverness also specializes in crochet work, while crocheted articles by Highland craft-workers are handled by Catherine of Inverness. Although the bulk of crochet work is conducted as a rural craft it would be invidious not to mention, in passing, the magnificent crochet work of Moira Podmore who works in Glasgow. She concentrates on larger items using fine crochet to produce all kinds of day and evening wear. Wool is the principal substance used in crochet, but cotton, silk and man-made fibres are also used extensively. Florence Stein of Knowepark Village in West Lothian makes a wide range of articles of clothing in different materials.

Compared with crochet, macramé was always a much more esoteric craft, practised desultorily by a few ladies in the nineteenth century, but with little indigenous tradition of an earlier date. Though the art of knotting stout twines and yarns into decorative articles of great beauty and complexity was known to the Arabs and other Mediterranean peoples a thousand years ago it did not come to the British Isles from Europe until the seventeenth century and, in fact, did not become widely popular in Scotland until the third quarter of the last century when it was enthusiastically applied to the making of lambrequins, chair-back covers, table mats and tidies for mantelpieces. It declined in popularity at the turn of the century and has only been revived to an appreciable extent within the past two decades. In its modern form macramé has been greatly extended, both in the variety of knots, and materials and in its application to such articles as belts and shopping bags. At first macramé craftsmen had to make do with the coarse twines and string traditionally associated with 'square knotting' (to use the older English expression), but in recent years a wide variety of special macramé threads has greatly increased the scope of this craft and fine, silky yarns are now used in the production of elegant macramé articles such as evening purses, wraps, stoles and jackets.

At a purely artistic level macramé knotting has imparted a three-dimensional quality to tapestry and wall-hangings, the greatest exponent of this technique being Dorothy Urquhart. At a humbler craft level, however, macramé is practised widely by the craftsmen who specialize in the fabric crafts of knitwear and crochet work. The outstanding exponent of macramé as an art applied to decorative garments is Glenda Marsh, whose work was exhibited in the Craftsman's Art Exhibition at the Victoria and Albert Museum in 1973. Fine macramé work is produced as a speciality of the Findhorn Studios of Forres.

[13]

Lapidary Work

The geology of Scotland, which contains some of the oldest rocks in the world, is surprisingly varied, and though no precious stones have yet been discovered there are many examples of semi-precious stones and hardstones which are most attractive when cut and polished. The best-known of the Scottish stones is cairngorm, a somewhat misleading name since *carn gorm* in Gaelic means 'green stone'. This smoky quartz which ranges in shade from pale straw to deep amber was traditionally associated with the Cairngorm Mountains and was originally mined in the veins of granite of Aberdeenshire. Cairngorms occurred in pebbles washed down from the Cairngorm mountains and found in the bed of the River Avon and the fast-flowing streams of Banffshire. They occur in many other parts of the country too: at Culblean on Deeside, at Usan near Montrose, in the hills of Kintyre, Galloway and Fife, and at Contin and Garve in Ross-shire. Dunrobin Glen near Golspie is another popular site. The quartz was cut and polished and much prized as a gemstone set in plaid brooches and the hilts of dirks. There is evidence to suggest that cairngorms were used in jewellery in medieval times, if not earlier.

There are also examples of reliquary brooches and caskets inlaid with other stones such as jasper, beryl and amethyst, but these stones never enjoyed the widespread popularity of cairngorm. Interest in the semi-precious stones of Scotland began to increase in the early years of the nineteenth century, but the prevailing fashion for jewellery in gold set with precious stones prevented widespread popularity. Boxes with inlays of semi-precious stones in the *zellenmosaik* style were produced at the turn of the century, and this technique was adapted to brooches and pendants, but pebble jewellery declined in popularity after 1910 until its revival in the 1950s. Amethyst, another form of tinted quartz which varies in colour from pale lilac to a rich reddish purple, is found in the mica schists of Perthshire, but also occurs in agate nodules at Usan and Scurdie Ness in Angus. Waterworn pebbles in the rivers and streams of Kirkcudbrightshire, particularly the Dee and the Urr, contain amethyst. It can also be found in the hills of Kintyre and at Kaim Hill near Largs in Ayrshire. Similarly, the cairngorm sites of Ross-shire and Sutherland also yield amethyst.

Chalcedony and colourless rock crystal are the other types of quartz widely distributed through Scotland, occurring in mineral veins in granite or in the pebbles washed down by mountain streams. Opaque quartz veins yield beryl and aquamarine. Sunstone is a combination of quartz and Orthoclase felspar found in many parts of Sutherland. Garnets, sometimes known as Scotch rubies, occur as well-formed crystals in the mica schists of Killin in Perthshire. Crystals large enough for cutting and faceting are rare, but smaller examples are relatively common and are used extensively as inlays in Scottish jewellery. They are widely distributed, but the main centres are at Elie Ness in Fife, at Contin and Garve in Ross-shire and in many parts of Sutherland, from Bettyhill and Kildonan to Struie. Jasper is an opaque stone found in shades of red, brown, yellow or green and occurs quite commonly in the ancient lava beds of Renfrewshire and the Clyde valley as well as on the island of Mull. Agates and carnelians occur as nodules in lava in many parts of Scotland, though are primarily associated with the Ayrshire coast between Heads of Ayr and Girvan. They may also be found on the coasts of Fife, Dunbar, Angus and at Ardmair Bay near Ullapool in Sutherland. Inland sites include the Pentland Hills near Carlops and the Ochil Hills at Path of Condie. Kyanite is a rare milky-blue mineral found in Banffshire.

The decorative potential of these minerals has long been recognized, but it is only since the Second World War that this has developed into an important craft. Today pebble jewellery is one of the most widespread crafts and makes use of many other stones for their distinctive pattern or texture in addition to the semi-precious stones enumerated above. The application of lapidary work to jewellery has already been discussed in Chapter 11, but it is interesting to note that both educational and aesthetic elements are involved and several of the craftsmen engaged in lapidary work specialize in presentation sets of geological specimens, both in their natural state and cut and polished. The Gem Rock Museum at Creetown combines the function of a museum dedicated to Scottish geology and a practical workshop where visitors may see stones being ground and polished.

Jewellery made on the premises as well as geological specimens are also available for sale to the public. Magnus Maximus Designs of Fort William and the Orcadian Stone Company of Golspie are the other leading distributors of geological specimens as well as hand-made jewellery. The Lapidary Workshops of Skene in Aberdeenshire and Sutherland Gemcutters of Achmelvich cater for the growing army of amateur lapidaries by providing them with mineral specimens, uncut stones or stones cut and polished for use by professional and amateur jewellers.

ORNAMENTAL STONEWORK

Scotland is rich in deposits of granite which has been exported all over the world. Creetown granite was used in the building of the Thames Embankment and London Bridge and in the form of tombstones has found its way to all corners of the globe. The granite quarries of the north-east brought mineral prosperity to that region long before the oil boom and Aberdeen's nickname of the Granite City is well-bestowed. Apart from its application to architecture and monuments, Scots granite is always associated with curling stones. This game is now universally popular but it originated in Scotland where the curlers were accustomed to use any reasonably flattish boulders from the river beds to skim across the ice of frozen rivers and ponds in winter-time. This sport had been played since time immemorial, with little regard to formal rules or the sizes and shapes of the stones, but by the middle of the eighteenth century some order was beginning to be instilled and gradually the weight, size and shape of the curling stones was regulated. Throughout the nineteenth century the sport continued unabated and with such refinements as indoor curling rinks it has now become an all-year-round activity. Its spread to other parts of the world has likewise stimulated the growth of the industry devoted to the cutting and polishing of curling stones whose picturesque names are derived from the places whence the granite is quarried – Ailsa Craig, Crawfordjohn, Carsphairn and Douglas Water being some of the commoner varieties. The granite is quarried and hewn into rough squares which are then sent to the makers for cutting and polishing into rounded stones weighing from thirty-five to forty-four pounds, set with iron and wooden handles. The cutting and polishing of curling stones is a traditional craft to which a new dimension has been added in recent years to meet the demands of the tourist industry. Today many of the country craftsmen making curling stones also produce half-size stones as doorstep ornaments, and even smaller versions, with silver handles, as desk ornaments or paperweights. The principal exponent of this is the Scottish Curling Stone Company of Inverness.

Serpentine, often though inaccurately described as a form of marble, is found in several parts of Scotland. In Tiree, Mull and Iona it is popularly known as Iona marble; in Perthshire it is known as Glen Tilt marble, from the river valley in which it occurs in spectacular veins in the river bed; and in Banffshire it is known as Portsoy marble, from the fishing village which is the centre of a specialized lapidary craft. It is found in workable quantities in other parts of the country, principally on the Ayrshire coast, round Lendalfoot and Ballantrae, and at Inchnadamph, Kylesku and Scourie in Wester Sutherland. Serpentine is an opaque stone with a smooth, waxy texture and a fine range of colouring from pale to dark green, red or brown, mottled and veined with white. It is now extensively used in the manufacture of Scottish pebble jewellery but it may also be found in larger items, such as cigarette and jewel boxes, table lighters, paperweights, ashtrays, lamp bases, desk sets, paperknives, penholders and mantel ornaments. The main workshops engaged in this craft are the Marble Workshop of Portsoy, Perthshire Crafts of Dunkeld, the Lapidary Workshop of Sandend near Portsoy and the Stone House of Avoch in Easter Ross. Jacken Products of Peterhead include a wide range of jewellery and objects of vertu made from serpentine and granite.

A fairly recent development has been the decoration of stones, rounded and smoothed by the natural action of the sea and the wind, in traditional Celtic or Norse designs. In many cases these pebbles, up to four inches in diameter, have the motif incised first and then colouring added to the grooves. In others the decoration is painted direct on to the smooth surface of the stones. The latter permits greater scope to the artist and includes small scenic vignettes and pictures of seals, salmon, Highland cattle and other subjects associated with the Highlands and Islands. Decorated stones, used as paperweights, are becoming very popular and because the basic materials are freely available they are to be found in craft shops all over the country.

[14]
Leather

This chapter is concerned with the use of animal skins after they have been tanned and dressed. There is today considerable application of untanned hides to the craft industries and this is discussed in Chapter 19. It is difficult, in an age of plastics and other man-made materials, to appreciate the paramount importance of leather in times past, not only as clothing but also as the medium for a wide variety of household and domestic articles: bottles, lamps, furniture, utensils, buckets and boats. In clothing alone, leather was the most versatile of substances and, particularly in the Highlands and Islands, it often took the place of woven cloth. Everything, from headgear to the stockings made from the skins of gannets, could be provided in leather of some form. Even to this day, leather plays a very prominent part in the costume and accessories of Highland dress.

The sporran developed out of the money pouch slung from the waist and common to many European peoples. As the ancient philibeg developed into the modern kilt, so also the sporran (which is merely the Gaelic word for a purse) underwent many transformations. Originally worn over the hip, it moved to a frontal position, and with this change of direction it became a much more ornamented item of apparel. It became larger and the original thongs which secured the flap became the decorative tassels – first consisting of elaborately knotted leather thongs, and then, in the nineteenth century, becoming the confection of bristles and silver mounts so beloved of the Victorians. At the same time other materials came into use. The simple cow-hide sporrans of earlier generations disappeared with the proscription of Highland dress, and when the ban was lifted the sporran emerged as an extremely decorated object made of sealskin, badger skin or even fox-hide, sometimes with the fox's mask mounted on the flap. Military sporrans of the nineteenth century were covered with horse-hair on a leather backing, with polished leather flaps, mounted in silver, complete with regimental insignia. When the original purpose of the thongs became lost, they developed into elaborate tassels and also increased in number. As many as six tassels festooned the front of the mid-nineteenth century sporran, though in more recent times the excesses of decoration have been largely eliminated. Elaborately mounted sporrans are still produced, though there is a tendency to return to the purer forms of the seventeenth and eighteenth centuries and to restrain the ornament to decorative tooling. Many of the animals which were previously sacrificed to provide the sporrans of the late Victorian era are now protected and cowhide is thus the main material used today, with deerskin a close second.

Apart from his sporran, the most distinctive dress accessory worn by the Highlander was his belt or belts. The waist-belt was a fearsome object of stout ox-hide, often up to four inches in breadth and almost an inch thick. Elaborate tooling and brass or silver studs decorated the waist-belt which was secured by an enormous buckle – again of brass or silver depending on the affluence of the owner. Traditional Celtic patterns decorated the belt and buckle. The cross-belt passed over the shoulder and terminated over one hip in a frog through which was secured the sword scabbard. Though generally thinner and narrower than the waist-belt, the cross-belt was also decorated in the traditional manner and secured by an ornate buckle at the middle of the chest. The more elaborate cross-belts even had attachments for knives and holsters for pistols. Both waist- and cross-belts declined in use after the Disarming Acts, and when the wearing of Highland dress was revived by the Lowland gentry in the 1820s these accessories appeared in a bastard form, generally far less robust and often more floridly embellished than the originals. At the same time a distinctive type of footwear was evolved which had little historic justification. Brogues (from Gaelic *brogan* – shoes) were largely a nineteenth-century invention. Traditionally Highlanders went barefoot or wore stockings made from the skins of wild birds and the idea of distinctive footwear probably did not arise until the first of the Highland regiments, the Black Watch, was raised to police the Highlands after the Jacobite Rebellion. The low, buckled shoes issued to Highland soldiers bore little resemblance to the elaborate brogues which became fashionable in the nineteenth century, with their tasselated thongs, fringed tongues and pierced patterns. Decorative brogues, for evening wear and a much stouter version for the grouse moors, have remained fashionable to this day and are largely machine-made, though a few leather craftsmen will produce fine hand-made brogues at a price.

The universal popularity of Highland dress, primarily for use by pipe bands, has made this aspect of leatherwork a major industry in Scotland. As a handcraft, however, it is still practised by R. Hodge of East Village, Pencaitland, who makes cross- and waist-belts, drum slings, flag-pole slings and harness associated with pipe bands.

SADDLERY AND BRIDLEWORK

The advent of the internal combustion engine began the decline in the usefulness of the horse, and the First World War almost killed it off entirely, but in the past two decades there has been a renaissance of horse-riding, and the development of the new sport of pony-trekking, both of which have stimulatd a revival of the ancient arts of saddlery and bridlework. Until well after the Second World War horses were still used extensively in many parts of Scotland for ploughing and for haulage, even in the towns and cities, and there was thus a steady demand for harness and halters. As this aspect of leatherwork has declined, the demand for saddlery has increased. Most of the country towns of Scotland can boast at least one saddlery firm whose craftsmen continue to practise skills handed down from generation to generation. This is a craft where mechanization has made little inroads and the work of cutting and stitching the leather is still largely done by hand.

Associated with saddlery and bridlework are the more ornamental crafts of game-bags and leather deer-stalking equipment. These sidelines of leathercraft developed steadily in the late nineteenth century when stag-hunting and grouse-shooting became fashionable among the upper class. Although these utilitarian aspects of leathercraft are now widely practised, the best examples are those produced by the Main family of Dunbar who also make the more decorative leather cases in addition to saddlery and game-bags.

TARGES

Leather as a protective covering for shields was widely known in ancient times and the Scots were among those peoples who continued to use leather shields long after such devices were abandoned elsewhere. The survival of shields in close combat may be explained by the fact that firearms played a relatively small part in Highland clan warfare. The last battle fought primarily with bows and arrows took place early in the seventeenth century, but thereafter the claymore, or Highland broadsword, was the principal weapon and it followed that the targe, or Highland shield, should be an important form of defence. The name was shortened from target (in Gaelic *targaid* is a shield) and denoted a circular shield up to two feet in diameter. Targes were made of two layers of wood, generally oak, with the grains crossed, covered by a layer of ox-hide up to an inch in thickness. The leather was secured to the wooden base by studs in a circular pattern round the edge and usually had a stout central boss. The vast majority of the targes actually wielded in anger would have conformed to this rudimentary pattern, but by the seventeenth century more decorative types had begun to appear. In these, pokerwork and tooling were applied to the leather and the studs were arranged in fancy designs, often capped by brass or even silver ornament. Great attention was paid to the central bosses, which may be found fluted or with a spiral motif, often ending in a sharp spike which could be used offensively as well as defensively. The most elaborate targes belonged to the early eighteenth century and had intricately cast ornament on the studs. These decorative targes belonged to a period when the pageantry of true Highland dress was at its zenith.

After the Jacobite Rebellion of 1745-6 targes joined other Highland accoutrements under government ban and when this was relaxed the need for targes had disappeared. In the nineteenth century, however, their decorative qualities led to their revival. The Highland targe became for Scotland what the copper and brass warming-pan became for England – a handsome wall ornament. As the supply of genuine Highland targes was understandably small, the reproduction of these shields developed into a minor Victorian industry which has continued to the present day. If anything, the modern craft of targe-making is truer to the original than the over-romanticized Victorian equivalent. Closer attention is now paid to the form and materials rather than the production of a purely decorateive item which would have been utterly impractical in clan fighting. These modern reproductions which follow the design and decoration of the seventeenth century rely on the qualities of the leathercraft and the restrained use of stud patterns for their decorative effect, and are more pleasing aesthetically on that account. Excellent replica targes are now being made by James

MacConnell of Inverness, Raymond Morris of Lochtayside Crafts near Aberfeldy and the Abbey Studios of Oldhamstocks in Berwickshire.

LEATHER SCULPTURE

The versatility of leather is seen at its best in the crafts of modelling and sculpture in this medium. The medieval process known as *cuir bouilli* (literally 'boiled leather'), which was used in the shaping of helmets, bottles and utensils, has been applied in more recent times to the moulding of leather for bicycle saddles but has also been extended into the realm of purely decorative leathercraft. Few leathers, other than modern chrome-tanned leather, can stand the effects of immersion in boiling water and the term is, in fact, applied to leather which is subject to heat at some stage in the modelling or moulding. More common, however, is the working of bas-reliefs on leather using the techniques of raised tooling. This was used in the production of bookbinding and sumptuous upholstery, but today it has been adapted to wall plaques, handbags, cigarette cases and belts. For this purpose leather with a supple, regular and flawless surface is preferred — usually sheepskin, calfskin or split cowhide. Raised tooling and *cuir bouilli* are employed in the production of heraldic plaques, historical figure studies and small sculptures by Andrew Barr of the Abbey Studios. Raymond Morris employs a combination of moulding, carving, incising, tooling and painting to produce decorative leather panels in Celtic designs. Increasing use is also being made nowadays of techniques borrowed from other countries, such as the type of leather embroidery practised by the Eskimos, or the braiding of rawhide as used by the Indians of the south-western United States. These techniques, allied to the more traditional European forms, impart great variety to the decorative leather panels now being produced in Scotland using Celtic or Norse traditional motifs.

LEATHER GOODS

The bulk of the leathercraft in Scotland consists of small articles such as gloves, belts, purses, handbags, keycases, pencil-cases, writing compendia and pocket books. Since leathercraft of this sort is now widely practised as a domestic pastime, and is taught in schools and evening classes, it is not surprising that this is one of the commonest of all the crafts. In many cases the production of small functional leather goods is carried on as a sideline to other crafts, such as pottery or weaving and it would be impossible to mention all the craftsmen and women who are engaged in this pursuit. The Garve Work Society of Garve in Wester Ross is an organization of craftworkers producing in their own homes a wide range of deerskin leather goods. Juniper Studios of Aldourie and Russcraft of Aviemore, both in Inverness-shire, specialize in hand-made leather goods. Hand-made leather boxes with tooled decoration, intended for use as jewel boxes or cigarette boxes, are a speciality of James Kirkwood of Pibroch Crafts, Crieff. Suede and leather bags, purses and articles of clothing are produced by Strathmore of Forfar, Lochside Gems of Fearnan and Lilian Thompson of Beith.

[15]

Metalwork

Traditionally, work in non-precious metals was largely carried on by village blacksmiths (working in wrought or beaten iron) and by the tinkers or *ceards* who went from place to place mending pots and pans. The craftsmen in non-ferrous metals formed part of the medieval Guild of Hammermen and included braziers, coppersmiths, pewterers and panel-beaters. Much of this traditional craftsmanship was swept away in the Industrial Revolution. The cheaper, mechanized products of the English Midlands drove out the age-old hand-made goods, and yet in the more remote parts of the country the village 'smiddy' continued to be a bastion of hand-wrought metalwork. Blacksmiths like the redoubtable John MacDonald of Ardvasar in Skye survived the lean years of the twentieth century to witness the rebirth of their ancient craft. Though many of these rural smithies had been transformed in the inter-wars years into garages and repair-shops, sufficient of the old skills of blacksmithing remained alive to form a useful nucleus for the more artistic forms of metalworking which have developed enormously in recent years. Credit for maintaining the traditional skills must go to the Royal Highland and Agricultural Society whose annual shows and competitions encouraged craftsmen to maintain an interest in wrought-ironwork. A few wealthy landowners, eschewing modern machine techniques, commissioned village craftsmen to make wrought-iron gates, door handles, railings and weathervanes. An unfortunate concomitant of the wartime drive for scrap metal was the destruction of much fine wrought-ironwork in Scottish towns and cities. With the passing of these fine gates and railings there also passed an appreciation for an art in which the Scots had long excelled. Today there are all too few examples of fine wrought-iron still *in situ*. Museum collections, however, are rich in wrought-iron and ironmongery of the past and there are indications that these excellent examples are now encouraging younger craftsmen to emulate them.

The renaissance of wrought-ironwork as an art began shortly

after the First World War when Thomas Hadden was commissioned by Lord Carmichael to fashion the wrought-iron gates and door furniture for Lennoxlove House near Stirling. Today this decorative ironwork is regarded as the equal of anything produced in the eighteenth century, the heyday of ornamental blacksmithing, and serves as a model for much of the ironwork produced in more recent times. Hadden himself is still active in this field and produces an enormous variety of wrought-ironwork from his workshop in Edinburgh. Much of the ornamental ironwork produced today, however, is wrought in small forges and smithies in the rural areas of Scotland. In some cases the more ornamental aspects of blacksmithing have developed out of an existing business which would formerly have been devoted largely to more utilitarian business. Such a smithy is that operated by E. Martin and Son at Closeburn in Dumfriesshire, where fine hand-forged ironwork has taken the place of the farrier-work of days gone by. Robert Marshall of Gateside Smithy near Beith, Ayrshire, William Watson of Carluke and George Stewart of Pitairlie Smithy in Newbigging near Broughty Ferry, Angus combine traditional blacksmithing and farrier-work with decorative wrought-ironwork.

Others have gone over almost entirely to ornamental metalwork. James Marshall of Bennybeg Smithy near Crieff specializes in the larger pieces, such as gates, grilles and railings. Much of the decorative ironwork is produced in the north of the country, ranging from the hand-wrought candlesticks and centre-pieces of the Balnakeil Forge at the Far North Craft Centre, to the ornamental metalwork of Stuart Fountain of Dornoch (who also produces copper and pewter jewellery and pewter tableware mentioned below). Ornamental Crafts of Ulbster in Caithness and James Thomson of Scalloway in Shetland produce a wide variety of wrought-ironwork, ranging from fire-irons and fire-dogs to candlesticks, from pin trays to plant stands, and also beaten metalwork plaques. Duncan MacMillan of Torlundy near Fort William specializes in screens of all shapes and sizes which he produces to commission, but also makes table and standard lamps and flowerpot holders. Roddy McKerracher and William Burns of Strathblane are among the more versatile craftsmen in metal, turning their hand to wrought-iron hearth furniture, beaten copperwork and even silver-etched jewellery.

COPPER AND PEWTER

Copper and its alloys, such as bronze, brass and spelter, have long been worked by Scottish craftsmen, but the design of Scottish copperware tended to be severely functional, with little thought for frills and frippery in ornament. Instead, the craftsmen turned out honest wares which relied entirely on their line and workmanship. Little historic copperware has survived and much of the hand-beaten copperware produced at the turn of the century is of rather dubious origin, since it relied on imported Art Nouveau motifs for ornamental effect. Modern hand-beaten copperware and brass tends to follow antique styles, and the kettles, pans, skillets and posnets are consciously designed as ornaments rather than for actual use. Various attempts are now being made to revive ancient utilitarian objects. The most promising example is the crusie or betty-lamp which in earlier times provided uncertain and malodorous illumination. The simple, heart-shaped pan and the delicately curved handle or wall-bracket of these crusies have captured the imagination of present-day craftsmen who have adapted this form to centre-pieces and plant or posy-holders, though this transformation in role has not been entirely happy.

Pewter was widely used in Scotland from the fifteenth to the nineteenth centuries and much of this survives to this day in such diverse forms as the communion plate, and tokens and measures such as the tappit hen, the chopin and the mutchkin. As in England, pewter declined in popularity in the second half of the nineteenth century as electroplate replaced it as a cheap and efficient substitute. At the same time, the increased output of pottery and bone china did away with the necessity for pewter drinking vessels and dishes. Today there are signs of a revival in pewtering, but mainly as a mechanized industry. Craft pewterware at the present time is being produced by Stuart Fountain of Dornoch and his excellent pewter tableware is an encouraging development.

Because of the toxic oxides associated with copper, this metal has never been suitable for utensils unless a coating of silver or tin is first applied. For this reason such copperware as is now produced by Scottish craftsmen tends more towards the fine arts. Bronze and copper wall plaques are among the repertoire of Bruce Weir of Jedburgh, who also produces wrought-ironwork. Clan crests in copper mounted on plastic are made by Roland Hill of Inverness. Decorative copperware by Norman Ruthven of

Clanart includes original paintings on copper plaques. Copper and pewter are, of course, more widely used in the manufacture of craft jewellery and are discussed in Chapter 11. The classical techniques of repoussage, beating and chasing are used in the production of copper and pewter plaques. Although bronze-casting and cold-casting are taught in the art colleges, there is little evidence as yet of a practical casting of figurines. David and Janet Miles of Scarista, Harris also produce cold-cast figures and chess pieces.

SCOTTISH WEAPONS

The continual state of lawlessness and clan warfare before the pacification of the Highlands in the second half of the eighteenth century is reflected in the wealth of arms produced in Scotland from 1500 to about 1790 and the distinctive styles of edged weapons and hand guns which evolved in that period. The principal weapon of the Highlander was the great sword (*claidheamh mòr*, anglicized as claymore), a monstrous, two-handed broadsword which would have been the direct descendant of the great sword wielded so devastatingly by Sir William Wallace in the thirteenth century. These giant swords are not to be confused with the Highland broadsword with its distinctive basket-hilt which developed in the seventeenth century and reached its zenith in the period between the two Jacobite Rebellions. This sword is often, though quite erroneously, called a claymore. The making of the basket-hilt combined the skills of wrought-metalwork, decorative inlay, casting, engraving and chasing. Very few hilts were decorated with gold or silver and the vast majority relied entirely on the skill of the hilt-maker for decorative effect. The blades themselves were usually imported from Scandinavia, the Low Countries, Italy or Spain as the Scots lacked the expertise in historical times to emulate the blade-makers of Toledo or the fabled Andrea Ferara whose name was often inscribed unscrupulously on blades to enhance their value. The other characteristic Scottish edged weapon was the *sgian dubh* (sometimes anglicized as skean dhu), an all-purpose dirk which was used as a parrying weapon, for stabbing and even as a piece of cutlery (often the only piece of cutlery) carried by the Highlander. Here again, the interest and value of Highland dirks lay mainly in the decorative treatment of the handle.

    Broadswords disappeared almost completely as a result of the

Disarming Acts, and survived only in an attenuated form as the weapon of officers in the Highland regiments. The *sgian dubh*, as has been previously noted, was revived as an ornamental accessory to the Highland dress which became fashionable in society from the 1830s onwards. Both broadswords and dirks are made to this day, though their manufacture is largely carried on in the English Midlands. As a craft, however, Scottish cut and thrust weapons have been revived in recent years and excellent hand-made swords and daggers are now being made again in the Highlands by James MacConnell of Inverness, Roy Matthews of Leslie, John Forsyth of Alva and Highland Armourers of Dornoch. Such weapons are also produced now by Bruce Weir of Jedburgh in the Borders. Miniature broadswords, suitable as paperknives or wall ornaments, are made by James Kirkwood of Pibroch Crafts, Crieff.

Scottish firearms have had a chequered career, the native industry having been virtually annihilated by fierce competition from the gunmakers of London and Birmingham. In their heyday, however, the Scottish gunsmiths, especially those who worked in the neighbourhood of Doune in Perthshire, were noted for their pistols which were unusual in having an all-metal construction. Scottish pistols, known as dags, were also distinctive in design, having rather longer barrels than their English counterparts and steel butts terminating in heart-shaped or double scroll finials which gave them a somewhat Moorish appearance sometimes enhanced by the use of silver or gold inlays. Relatively few pistols were decorated so extravagantly, and the majority of them relied on the quality of the steel itself, the precision of the action and the balanced proportions of their design.

The all-metal construction of Scottish pistols has attracted the attention of metalworkers in recent years. Replica Highland dags are now being made by several of the craftsmen already mentioned: and, in addition, miniature cannon based on the celebrated 'Mons Meg' and other pieces of historic ordnance are now being made by Robert Drysdale of Bannockburn.

[16]

Musical Instruments

The musical instrument which is most readily identified with Scotland all over the world is the bagpipes. Although Scottish pipes are now played in every corner of the globe, from Canada to New Zealand, from Nepal to Uganda – by bands tricked out in tartan finery to match – the bagpipes are not essentially a Scottish instrument at all. There is ample evidence, from statuary, illuminated manuscripts and woodcuts, to suggest that some form of bagpipes was played all over Europe in the Middle Ages and it is something of a mystery that in Scotland alone this primitive instrument should have developed and attained international recognition. Admittedly bagpipes of a sort are played in other countries, including the Balkans and Ireland, and have maintained their individuality to this day, but none of these variants has achieved the distinction and the worldwide acclaim of the Scottish pipes.

The Scottish bagpipes as we know them today, are largely an invention of the past two centuries and the standardization of design is much more recent than that. The earliest pipes, dating from medieval times, possessed only one drone. A second drone was added in the sixteenth century and a third about the middle of the eighteenth, although one- or two-drone sets of pipes were still made in the nineteenth century. Bagpipes in themselves combine several ancient crafts. The bag was fashioned from sheepskin, the pipes were exquisitely turned from blocks of box or hawthorn and the terminals carved from bone. The joints and mountings were made of silver and often intricately chased with Celtic decoration. Finally the drones were held in place by braided tasselled cords and the bag was covered with woven tartan cloth, following the sett of the piper. Thus leathercraft, wood-turning, bone-carving, silversmithing and weaving were involved. Today the bulk of bagpipe manufacturing is conducted in Edinburgh or Glasgow so it can scarcely be regarded as a rural craft, although the making of bagpipes is a skilled job, involving a high proportion of handcraft and practised by men who often inherited these skills from their forbears. Invitably the fascination which the bagpipes wield on tourism has led to the development of miniature bagpipes which, though producing music of a sort, are intended primarily as souvenirs of Scotland.

Of comparable antiquity with the bagpipes are the various stringed instruments which, having been neglected for many years, are now enjoying something of a revival. The Scottish harp or clarsach has, perhaps, been overshadowed by the other Celtic versions of this instrument associated with Ireland and Wales, but over a thousand years ago the clarsach was the most honoured of Scottish instruments, at a time when bagpipe-playing was regarded as no more than the pastime of shepherds. Harpers enjoyed a privileged place in feudal society and clarsachs are numbered among the greatest antiquities of Scotland. The ancient Scottish harp, however, gradually lost ground to continental innovations such as the lute and the violin, and seems to have disappeared altogether in the early eighteenth century. Its revival in the 1890s was purely academic, a manifestation of that renewed interest in anything pertaining to the golden age of Celtic romanticism. Lord Archibald Campbell, pioneer of the Clarsach Society, commissioned Glen's of Edinburgh (still in the forefront of bagpipe manufacture) to produce three clarsachs, modelled on those preserved in the National Museum of Antiquities, and from this original trio stem all the other clarsachs which have been produced in many parts of Scotland over the past eighty years.

It should be noted that, although the revival of the clarsach at the turn of the century was the most dramatic, interest in other forms of stringed instrument was keen at the same time. The late nineteenth century was a period in which piano-makers turned their hands to such instruments as zithers and dulcimers, mandolines and lutes, banjos and guitars. Many of these stringed instruments were made by enthusiastic amateurs rather than skilled craftsmen, and the quality of workmanship in these old instruments often leaves much to be desired. The same is true of the many variations on the violin which were made up and down the country from the middle of the nineteenth century onwards. Some of these Scottish fiddles, with triangular or rectangular bodies, seem unbelievably crude by comparison with the elegant lines of a Cremona violin though these were the instruments on which Scottish fiddlers played their reels and jigs for countless generations.

The revival of interest in old instruments at the turn of the century led to the production of some unlikely hybrids, such as the cellamba (a combination of cello and the ancient viol de gamba) or even the lutar (whose uneasy parents were the medieval lute and the eighteenth-century Spanish guitar). The appearance of these strange hybrids was occasioned by a genuine desire to take the ancient instruments forward in development to that point which they might have attained had they not been allowed to go out of fashion. Since the Second World War, however, there has been an increasing tendency to get back to first principles and to construct instruments which are true to the ancient originals. It would be difficult to estimate the extent of the present craft of musical instruments in Scotland. Dr Ian Firth of St Andrews, himself one of the outstanding makers of clarsachs and lutes in Scotland today, has estimated that there are at least 600 makers of musical instruments. Like enamelling, lapidary work and soft toy-making, this is a craft which has also become widely popular as a pastime. There are, as yet, few craftsmen who are engaged in the making of musical instruments as a full-time occupation. In this category come Messrs Sanderson and Taylor of Alva in Clackmannanshire, who make all kinds of stringed instruments, from clarsachs to harpsichords, William Sampson of Carnoustie who makes lutes, and Atholl Harpsichords of Blair Atholl in Perthshire who both make and repair harpsichords and clavichords.

[17]

Pottery

Although pottery of a sort must have been produced in Scotland since the earliest times it did not develop beyond the most primitive forms and the requirements of the immediate locality until the eighteenth century. Functional pottery, including both tiles and tableware, was produced in a number of small potteries mainly situated around the east coast where the influence of the Low Countries rather than England was most marked. There are numerous eye-witness accounts of the pottery made at Leith, Bo'ness, Prestonpans, Portobello and other places round the Firth of Forth in the late seventeenth and early eighteenth centuries. John Ray's account of glass-making at Prestonpans in 1661 mentions the crucibles made from local pipe-clay, pointing to a high level of technical competence in the Scottish pottery of that period. It was not until 1696, however, that the manufacture of pottery began on a large scale for domestic usage in Prestonpans. Subsequently other potteries in the neighbourhood concentrated on pipes and tiles and in the mid-eighteenth century it is believed that fine china was also being made in the vicinity of Musselburgh, allegedly 'in the manner of Bow and Chelsea'.

On the west coast the most prominent pottery was that established in Glasgow in 1748, the site being appropriately named Delftfield (between Anderston and the Broomielaw). As the name implies this pottery concentrated on the production of tin-glazed delftware, of a type which had previously been manufactured in Lambeth, Liverpool and Bristol, and in techniques, materials and personnel the Delftfield works relied heavily on English expertise. Although the Delftfield pottery established a flourishing export business, supplying North America with household wares both before and after the War of Independence, it could not compete with the cheaper wares which flooded Scotland from Staffordshire in the early nineteenth century and by 1820 it had gone out of business. Very few examples which can definitely be assigned to the Delftfield pottery appear to have survived. Another of the early Scottish potteries was at Verreville which, as its name suggests, was

originally noted for its glassworks. The Verreville works at
Finnieston turned from crystal glass to earthenware and though it
was long credited with the manufacture of porcelain, this has
now been discounted. In the second half of the nineteenth
century it produced a vast amount of ironstone and this
continued until the First World War when the business ran
down and was finally closed in 1918. By the late nineteenth
century there were many other commercial potteries in the
Central Lowlands of Scotland. In the Glasgow area alone were
Bell's, the Britannia Pottery at St Rollox, the Campbellfield
Pottery, the Possil Pottery (famed for its 'Nautilus' porcelain)
and the Victoria Pottery at Pollokshaws. On the east coast there
were Gordon's, Watson's and Bellfield in the Prestonpans
district, the Bo'ness Pottery and several smaller works in the
Kirkcaldy area run by the Heron and Methven families.
Altogether there were over a hundred small potteries in
operation in Scotland in the nineteenth century, but many of
them were overtaken by the rapid industrial expansion and the
growth of the cities which spread out over the surrounding
countryside.

The bulk of their wares consisted of domestic and table wares,
tiles and, latterly, sanitary ware. At one time a considerable
amount of decorative earthenware, from pirley pigs (piggy
banks) to wally dugs (china dogs), was also produced, but this
relatively unsophisticated pottery lost ground to English and
German imports. Before the onslaught of Staffordshire flatback
figures and Saxon china fairings the native 'dabbities' and slip-
decorated saut buckets and butter-dishes stood little chance. By
the turn of the century there was comparatively little evidence of
artistry in Scottish pottery and output was concentrated on
industrial and useful wares. It is surprising that the influence of
the Glasgow school, led by Mackintosh, MacNair and the
MacDonald sisters, was not felt on pottery to any extent. There
was no tradition of studio pottery in Scotland as there was in
England, and the small pottery operated by Hugh Allan on the
banks of the river Allander between 1904 and 1908 seems to have
been the only one which concentrated solely on decorative wares.
Allan developed some highly distinctive coloured glazes, curdled
by the addition of raw oxides of tin and other metals, and also used
crystalline enamels. Allan's pottery is now comparatively rare,
though it is well documented by the examples which he presented
to the Glasgow Museum and Art Galleries at Kelvingrove.

The artistic approach to pottery in Scotland was at its nadir in the years immediately before the First World War. Yet this was the period in which the Tollcross pottery, known as Govancroft, was established and which continues to this day to produce fine stoneware. Craft pottery as such, however, is a development of the past decade and the growth of this rural industry in recent years has been nothing less than dramatic. At the present time there are about a hundred small studio potteries in operation, but the number is increasing every year. Although the art colleges have been responsible for much of this development a high proportion of the craftsmen involved are not of Scottish origin, but have migrated from England, Europe and America. Significantly, the only truly indigenous craft pottery to have survived into the present century was produced of necessity for the use of the crofters in the remoter districts of the Isle of Lewis. Bearing in mind that the products of the English potteries had found their way to the remotest inhabited island of them all – St Kilda – by the 1890s, it seems hard to imagine why other parts of the Hebrides should have been forced to rely on home-made crocks and bowls. But St Kilda was the *ultima Thule* of the late-Victorian and Edwardian tourist, whereas places nearer the mainland, such as Lewis and Eriskay, were little frequented. At Barvas in Lewis a very crude pottery of a greyish-slate colour was produced as late as the 1920s. It was utterly devoid of finish or glaze, and though robust in appearance (because of its thickness) it was actually rather fragile since the primitive kilns in which it was fired could not produce the required heat. These unbelievably crude pieces of Barvas pottery nonetheless had a sculptural quality which hand-thrown pottery seldom possesses.

The potters of Barvas were simple men who plied their craft as a sideline to fishing and farming and employed techniques and skills (if they could be thus described) which had been transmitted from generation to generation for hundreds of years. There is, in Barvas pottery, a striking affinity with the fragments of pottery which have been recovered from archaeological sites all over northern Europe dating back to Neolithic times.

The craggy, misshapen quality of Barvas pottery is far removed from the work produced today by potters, often working in places just as remote. The difference is that the craftsmen of the present time are working in remote areas from choice. It is a matter for conjecture how far the reaction against mechanization and urban living has influenced the modern craft potters. In some cases they have selected a site which is convenient for distinctive local clays, but more often than not craft potters rely on suppliers in the Central Lowlands or even in England. Moreover, although a few idealists are working with primitive kilns or simple open firing, the majority employ modern, electrically fired kilns. Given the high quality and consistency of materials supplied by specialists in this field and the technical virtuosity of electrically operated wheels and kilns, it is not surprising that much of the pottery made today is of a very high standard in finish though perhaps lacking in inspiration and originality.

This is not to deny that there is tremendous variety in Scottish craft pottery which ranges from the purely functional tablewares and slipcast wares, through hand-thrown earthenware and stoneware to coiled pots and the most *avant-garde* structures which are more sculptural than functional. Interest in Scottish pottery in recent years has stimulated the formation of the Scottish Pottery Society which, while not confined to Scottish ceramics, far less those of the present day, has inevitably encouraged an appreciation of what is happening now. In addition, and probably of greater significance to the progress of the craft, is the formation recently of the Scottish Craft Potters Association which provides a forum for the interchange of ideas between the craftsmen and also permits interested laymen to become more closely involved with the ceramic arts and crafts.

STONEWARE

Following the example of the craft potters in England, active since the end of the First World War, the Scottish potters have until recently shown a marked preference for stoneware, a type of pottery distinguished from the softer earthenware by its hardness and the texture of its surface. Technically, stoneware differs mainly from earthenware in the firing at a much higher temperature (between 1100°C and 1280°C). Salt-glazing is the method most commonly used, the variation in texture and colour of the glaze being determined by the quantity of salt thrown into the kiln at the glazing stage. From the customer's viewpoint, stoneware is generally more robust than earthenware and not so liable to chipping or flaking. The disadvantage of stoneware is the rather limited range of colours – mostly browns and sombre hues of green or blue. Nevertheless the delicate tonal qualities of stoneware glazes and the almost lustrous appearance which is sometimes achieved have attracted the attention of many potters who continue to concentrate on this form of ceramics. Variety is imparted in the use of coloured glazes decorated in wax resist, a technique used by John Davey of Bridge of Dee in Kirkcudbrightshire to great effect in his larger pieces, such as bowls, platters and lamp-bases.

Hand-thrown stoneware pots are produced by numerous craftsmen, and it seems invidious to select a few examples. Among those who have specialized in this medium, for domestic wares – plates, bowls, butter-dishes, tea and coffee sets and jugs – are Shirley Bracewell of Drymen, Bob Park of Culloden Pottery, David Drewery of the Ardfern Pottery, Joan Faithfull of Eskbank, Stephen Grieve of the Crail Pottery, Stewart Johnston of Dess Station Pottery, Thomas Lochhead of the Old Mill Pottery in Kirkcudbright, Donald Logie of the Wellbrae Pottery in Errol, Sheila McNaught of Callander, Graham McVitie of Tynehead, Midlothian, Irene Morton of the Farmhouse Pottery, Minishant, Bill Edmond and Jack Dawson of the Peebles Pottery and Mrs Fischer Young of Tayport. Alexander Leckie, better known nowadays for his individual sculptural pieces, also produces stoneware pots. The more decorative stoneware pieces are a speciality of Anne Lightwood of Lower Largo. Carolina Valvona of Newbridge, Midlothian is one of the few potters currently experimenting with coloured glazes in stoneware. Probably the best-known exponent of stoneware and redclay in domestic and tablewares is Barbara Davidson of Larbert whose astonishing output ranges from coffee cups and mugs to casseroles, tureens, punch bowls and other larger items. Mike Jordan of the Gaitgill Pottery, Twynholm, has adapted the type of stoneware one usually associates with drainpipes and evolved some interesting forms, of which his bee-hive cheese-dish and cover is the most noteworthy. Within the limited range of colours available stoneware is decorated by contrasting bands of brown, grey and cream and this is seen at its most effective in the smaller cylindrical objects, such as vases and beakers. This technique of 'layering' contrasting bands of muted shades is used by Gretl Shapiro of Earra Gael, and is seen at its most effective in her tall slender stoneware decanters and matching wine beakers. Stoneware with carved Celtic motifs is produced by Pat Laurenson of Scalloway, Shetland.

EARTHENWARE

Under this heading comes all manner of pottery fired at temperatures below 1100°C and ranging from articles with a matt, biscuit surface (terracotta) to those with highly coloured glazes and lustre decoration. Much of the variety imparted to earthenware lies in the glazes based on metallic oxides, woodash, enamels, glass or contrasting forms of clay. A fundamental difference between craft pottery and the factory-made earthenware today is that the latter is predominantly cast whereas the former is invariably thrown on a wheel. Slip-casting by hand is seldom suitable for adaptation to larger items, though this technique is ideal for small figures and ceramic jewellery requiring a three-dimensional appearance. Slip-cast models and pendants are a speciality of the Glen Tanar Pottery. Slip – a mixture of clay and water with a creamy consistency – is ideal as a decorative medium applied to the sides of vessels thrown or modelled in clay of a different colour or stiffer consistency. A wide range of decorative slipware is produced by Anne Lightwood of Lower Largo and John Miller of the Ferryport Pottery in Fife. The oustanding pieces from the Ferryport Pottery include tureens and fruit bowls with intricate ornament and inscriptions applied in thin trails of slip in contrasting colours. Slipware, both slipmoulded and slip-decorated earthenware, is made by the Cromarty Design Workshop of Fishertown, who have enormous variety of sizes, shapes and ornamental motifs.

Earthenware, with its much lighter body and infinite variety of glazes and colours, provides the greatest scope for the present-day potters. Two of the largest craft potteries now operating in rural Scotland produce a wide range of hand-thrown pottery. Castlewynd Studios of Inverdruie near Aviemore have concentrated on useful domestic and tablewares, reviving traditional forms such as coggies (shallow bowls with a handle at right angles) and saut buckets, but their repertoire also includes more orthodox forms such as mugs, vases and decorative plates. The characteristic feature of Castlewynd pottery is its brilliant white matt glaze decorated with contrasting bands of yellow, ochre, browns, purples, blues and green merging almost impercetibly into each other. The coggies, which are ideal as dessert plates or porridge bowls, are irregular and asymmetrical in both the bowl and handle, whereas the coggies produced by the Pypers Wynd pottery in Prestonpans, though hand-thrown, have an almost machine precision about them, both bowls and handles being perfectly regular. Pypers Wynd pottery is decorated in glazes with predominantly yellow and brown shades. The temptation to embellish their wares with thistle motifs has proved too much, and unfortunately they are not alone in descending to this type of 'schmaltz'.

The Old Kirk pottery at Kilmun, operated by Z. Predavec, also concentrates on tableware, using a white glossy glaze tinged with blue. A distinguishing feature of Old Kirk pottery is its bands of applied decoration in quasi-Celtic scrollwork, usually picked out in a contrasting colour. The white surface is usually decorated with underglaze transfer prints of Scottish subjects. Much of the Old Kirk pottery consists of vases, jam-pots and beer mugs aimed at the middle spectrum of the tourist trade. The Thistle Pottery was formerly based in Portobello, one of the traditional pottery centres of Scotland, but in recent years has moved to Crieff in Perthshire. The vast repertoire of this pottery ranges from small butter dishes to outsize whisky jars. As its name implies, this pottery had a predilection for Scotland's national floral emblem as a decorative motif, and this, in full natural colours against muted grey-blue grounds, characterizes much of their earlier wares, though more recent pottery has broken away from this tradition and has much freer decorative treatment, often tending towards the abstract.

Orr Ceramics of Lybster in Caithness produce both domestic pottery and figures. The former are characterized by white glazes against which stand out relief decoration in the biscuit colour of the body. This technique is seen at its most effective in the more two-dimensional subjects, such as plates, butter-dishes and ashtrays, though it is also applied to the sides of mugs and vases. The Isle of Lewis pottery in Great Bernera makes earthenware with a pale cream body decorated with a distinctive honey-brown glaze. Relief ornament appropriate to the subject is often added to the lids of honey-pots, the bottoms of butter-dishes and so on. The Craw pottery of Lochranza in Arran produces domestic and small ornamental wares with a pale, speckled blue glaze decorated with motifs derived from nature.

Redclay ware is made by several Scottish craft potteries and is distinguished by the reddish colour of the body, varying from the bright brick shade of the Craigdhu pottery and some of the pottery produced by Peter Layton at Morar, to the deep shades of jasper found in the Crail pottery and the McIver pottery of Moniaive. The latter uses distinctive glazes of deep brown and green which possess a slightly iridescent quality.

Muriel and Gordon Macintyre of the Nairn pottery made earthenware with sgraffito decoration, but have also turned their attention to majolica, a type of pottery which was very fashionable at the turn of the century in jugs, mugs, vases and tiles. Majolica is characterized by its relief decoration coated with brilliantly coloured glazes produced from metallic oxides. Among the more unusual styles to have emerged so far is that evolved by Gerard Lyons of Moffat whose smaller pieces often incorporate fused glass in shades of green and blue. His larger wares, such as vases and plant-pot holders, have a distinctive creamy matt exterior decorated with vigorous whorls and bands of deep brown, with a dull-brown or green glaze on the interior.

Most of the pottery referred to above is thrown on a wheel, but a few potters also specialize in slabware, in which the clay is rolled out into slabs. These are then cut into sections which, when joined together, make up pots and vases with a box format. The components are allowed to set a little so that they are more easily handled and will stand upright. Clay slip is used to join the pieces. A greater variety of shapes can be achieved by forming the slabware over a plaster mould which then absorbs the moisture from the clay, causing it to shrink away from the mould. This technique is known as press-moulding and is sometimes used to make vases, spill-holders, caddies and boxes. Slabware is currently being made by Cromarty Design Workshop, Joan Faithfull of Eskbank, Stewart Johnston of Dess Station pottery, Findhorn Studios and Mrs Fischer Young of Tayport. Some slabware is overdecorated, but it is heartening to observe that the Scottish potters have achieved a fine balance of decoration and shape in their slabbed pots.

PORCELAIN

Sometimes described as the most precious of man-made objects, this form of ceramics compounded of china clay and felspathic stone requires firing at a temperature between 1300°C and 1500°C. Because of the relatively high cost both of materials involved and the equipment required, very few craft potters have been working in this exacting medium. Among those which have so far ventured into this field are the Bongate Studio pottery of Jedburgh, the Bute pottery in Rothesay, the Nairn pottery and Leslie Yeoman of Skye. The porcelain bowls and dishes produced by Miss Yeoman have an unusual, sculptural quality imparted by their irregular shape and the novel use of double or treble walls of thin porcelain joined at irregular intervals. As functional pieces it would be hard to imagine anything less practical, and yet these dishes have a charm and originality which is seldom present in the more orthodox functional wares.

DECORATIVE AND INDIVIDUAL PIECES

The great bulk of the pottery now being produced in Scotland comes under the heading of functional, domestic and tablewares or small and relatively low-priced decorative items which are still primarily functional – ashtrays, sweetmeat dishes, butter-dishes, candle-holders, egg-cups, mugs and beakers. Although most of the latter rely on the quality and striation of the glazes for decorative effect, relief, slip-trailed or enamel-painted motifs abound and ornament in wax resist is occasionally used. Most potters are forced by the economic facts of life to concentrate on 'bread and butter' items, which can be turned out rapidly and can be retailed at a price to suit the pocket of the average tourist. It would be interesting to speculate on the total retail value of the ordinary wares now produced and sold each year and it is not improbable that the turnover of functional pottery far exceeds the revenue from purely decorative and sculptural pottery. The collector who also has a shrewd eye on investment will be more interested in the larger, more expensive, individual works and this is the area in which that undefinable quality of genius begins to take over from mere technical excellence. No doubt most of the potters already mentioned have ambitions to devote more time to individual pieces, and as they make the grade in the more commercial lines they will undoubtedly concentrate on the larger works which are more rewarding both to the potter and the purchaser. One of the exciting aspects of Scottish crafts pottery at the present time is that it is still in its adolescence. There are, of course, a number of potters whose names have already become established and whose works now command high prices which the discerning public is only too ready to pay; but there are others whose individual pieces are as yet little more than a sideline to their functional wares and thus afford scope to the collector willing to gamble on the future reputation of such up and coming potters.

Ceramics provide the nearest approach to the fine arts in any field of the crafts today and, indeed, it is often difficult to differentiate between sculpture and some of the more experimental pieces conceived purely as decorative items. Pottery is one of the most glamorous of the craft media and tends to dominate the craft exhibitions. A third of the exhibits at the first Craft Biennale in 1974 (57 out of 170) were of pottery, the largest single medium on display, and the same ratio is evident in other general exhibitions both in the art colleges and in international shows such as the Craftsman's Art Exhibition at the Victoria and Albert Museum in 1973.

At the moment a spirit of compromise prevails, and many potters, both established artists like David Cohen or David Heminsley, and those whose output is geared mainly to domestic wares, concentrate their creative talents on objects which are both decorative and functional. Thus lamp-bases, vases, umbrella stands, plant-pot holders and platters are the principal vehicles for artistic expression. These comparatively large pieces offer the opportunity for the individual craftsman to try out his theories on glazing, and to evolve distinctive – not to say idiosyncratic – styles of ornament, while still offering the public articles which fulfil some readily apparent function. The most disheartening question overheard at exhibitions and trade fairs is 'But what does it actually *do*?'

One would need a separate volume to do justice to the ceramic arts in Scotland, so any discussion of individual decorative wares must be selective. Hilda Brown of the Lussagiven pottery in the island of Jura has ignored domestic wares almost entirely and concentrates on a range of ceramic fairy-tale castles of varying shapes and sizes which make striking centre-pieces or free-standing ornaments. Architecturally these pieces are unlike anything to be found in Scotland (or England either, for that matter) and they have an ethereal quality redolent of illustrations from the Brothers Grimm. Peter Beard and Alan Nairn, who have joined forces in the Glenmoriston pottery, produce vases with squat gourd-like bodies surmounted by foliate excrescences on narrow stalks, giving them a singularly plant-like appearance. The rough texture of these vases and the irregular, almost ragged edges of their lips deliberately heighten the analogy with the vegetable world.

David Cohen, now working at Craggan Mill near Grantown-on-Spey in partnership with the glass-blower, Ron Boyco, is one of the most prominent potters in Scotland today. His name is a household word wherever fine modern ceramics are appreciated, and his one-man exhibitions attract a ready audience. He is also one of the most versatile ceramicists whose mastery of materials and glazes has produced work which is exciting and intriguing from both visual and tactile angles. Among his more functional pieces may be mentioned the tall, slender whisky jars and wine decanters, the elaborate, almost Oriental teapots, his vases with their fat bodies and narrow necks, casseroles and punch-bowls. His stoneware is fired at very high temperatures, almost approaching those required for porcelain, and the delicate appearance of his work belies its essential toughness. Like many of his contemporaries, Cohen has gone back to nature for inspiration and this is reflected in his decorative motifs in which hills, trees and cloud formations are recurring themes. The vivid colouring of his glazes is often contrasted with black and gold borders, though the sombre combination of black and gold is sometimes used exclusively on jugs and urns of funereal intensity. Even his smaller and relatively inexpensive pieces, such as candle-holders and ceramic bells possess that delicacy of shape and mastery of glazes which characterize his individual works.

Alasdair Dunn trained as a sculptor and his work might more accurately be described as ceramic sculpture rather than pottery in the craft sense. The nearest that he comes to conventional pottery is in his vases, but even these are modelled in such a way as to defy employment in the orthodox manner, though a few of them have been pierced so that they can be used as the basis for dried flower arrangements. His other work falls into two main categories which he describes as wheel sculpture and 'chuckie-stanes' respectively. The wheel sculptures are two-dimensional relief panels or three-dimensional standing forms which vaguely resemble trees. Two distinctive types of clay are used in these wheel sculptures – a richly flecked stoneware body and a striated body in which clays of contrasting colours have been banded together. The sculptures consist of variations on a theme involving fan-like convolutions spreading out of the top of cylindrical masses. The chuckie-stanes derive their name from the familiar Scottish expression for pebbles worn smooth by the action of sea and river and exhibiting banding and striation. Dunn's pebble forms are, in fact, enlargements of this natural phenomenon and were inspired by the patterns found on the stones littering the beaches and river-beds of Arran where he has his studio. Clays of different colours are combined (like the so-called agate ware which was popular in certain English potteries a century ago) and pounded into a mass which, when thrown on the potter's wheel, produces an infinite variety of striation. These chuckie-stanes are hollow and glazed inside and in many cases the glazes have been deliberately allowed to run out of the top and down across the outside to contrast with the banding and speckling of the coloured clays. The sides of these pebble forms are pierced to hold dried grasses, bullrushes and other types of dried vegetation. In some of his ceramic sculpture Dunn has combined clay with pieces of driftwood to produce abstracts.

Alison and Nigel Gow formerly in Kelso but now at the Blackadder Pottery in Westruther Gordon, Berwickshire, have produced a fine range of decorated pots and vases of all shapes and sizes, but their principal forte consists of wall plaques creating a *trompe l'oeil* effect. These plaques resemble windows, framed with lace curtains and pelmets, looking out on to Scottish street scenes. In the foreground is a window ledge on which often sits a dish or a cup (adding a three-dimensional touch). More recently they have been making pottery cottages giving a modern slant to the nineteenth-century cottage pastille burners which were popular with the Staffordshire potters.

David Heminsley is a good example of the more cosmopolitan craftsmen now working in Scotland. Educated in Birmingham, he lectured in ceramics at the Ulster College of Art and Design before moving from Belfast to Scotland and becoming a founder member of the Balbirnie Craft Centre. His wife Marjorie trained at the Ulster College and is a dress designer and maker of fashion goods. Although Heminsley produces the full range of domestic and functional wares, from condiment sets and egg cups to mugs and dishes in oxidized stoneware fired at a very high temperature, his most notable work consists of very large ornamental pots, lamp-bases, plant-holders and vases, with elaborate incised decoration. His most striking work, however, is his suspended ceramic sculpture, much of which is pierced to hold dried flower arrangements.

Ian and Elizabeth Hird, both graduates of the Edinburgh College of Art, founded the Kelso Pottery in August 1970 and had the first kiln in Scotland to be fired by natural gas. They produce domestic stoneware with a distinctive, speckled, reddish-brown glaze, but from the outset they were also preoccupied with the more artistic aspects of ceramics. Both in techniques and decorative expression there is a Japanese quality about their work. Raku firing in the Japanese manner is now used to create those soft, fluid effects in the glazes on pots and platters decorated with a deceptively simple style and economy of line which might suggest the influence of Hamada – except that the austere landscapes, relieved only by occasional clumps of trees, are in fact typical of the broad, rolling countryside of the Borders. The influence of the hills and trees of Roxburghshire can also be seen in the relief decoration on many of their larger pots. These have only a limited range of colours and rely on their form and texture for decorative effect.

Alexander Leckie graduated from the Glasgow School of Art, went to Australia where he successively worked in a ceramics factory in Adelaide, taught at the South Australia Art School and eventually had his own ceramics studio where he developed a style of highly intricate stoneware whose decoration was subconsciously influenced by ancient Mexican and Peruvian art. This pottery was a unique blend of earthenware and stoneware, being both incised and painted and requiring up to five firings. He returned to Scotland in 1966 to head the ceramics department at the Glasgow School of Art and eight years later established his own studio again in the Stirlingshire countryside to the north of Glasgow. Like his contemporaries Leckie was forced into domestic pottery because that is what is commercially viable, though all the time he hankered to return to the higher levels of ceramic art which he had practised in Australia. His most recent work is pure ceramic sculpture in which painting has become an essential ingredient. He has now reached the stage where painting and sculpture are overlapping and intermingling and at one extreme one may consider his pottery as a form of three-dimensional painting combined with all kinds of other materials. Even his pots which are still recognizable as vessels of some kind have this sculptural painting quality; typical examples of this are his wine bottles built on three stout legs, with lavishly painted and coruscated surfaces.

Robert Park trained at Harrogate Art College and the Bath Academy of Art before migrating to Invernessshire. He established a small pottery at Culloden Moor, hence the name of Culloden Pottery which he still uses, although he moved some two years later to his present location at the Old Smiddy in Gollanfield, just off the main road between Inverness and Nairn. Inevitably a large proportion of his output consists of domestic earthenware and stoneware, but he has also produced some highly distinctive individual pieces. Much of his pottery is thrown, though some larger pieces are built up by the ancient technique of coiling 'snakes' of clay. This method (which is still used in many parts of Africa to this day) has enabled Park to produce some very large pots. A characteristic feature of his work is the extensive use of applied decoration which ranges from a recurring motif of a squared circle or wheel pattern to all-over motifs which suggest the action of wind and weather or stone etched into highly convoluted patterns. In form he has a preference for intricate vase or bowl shapes surmounting tall, slender stems and plain bases.

There are many other potters at present endeavouring to produce the more decorative kinds of ceramics in addition to useful wares: Dion Alexander of the Colonsay Pottery, Jack Dawson and Bill Edmond of the Peebles Pottery, Stephen Grieve of the Crail Pottery, Anne Lightwood of Lower Largo, Donald Logie of the Wellbrae Pottery, Gerard Lyons of the Moffat Pottery, John Miller of the Ferryport Pottery, Donald Swan of the Isle of Cumbrae Pottery and Robert Waddell of Gordonstoun are all making individual pieces of considerable artistic merit. Both David Illingworth of the Far North Pottery at Balnakeil and Peter Layton at Morar have already produced much pottery which veers towards sculpture in its form. Rozelle Holden of Calderstone in Lanarkshire is experimenting with unusual glazes and surface texture in her stoneware pots and vases – here again we may also see the vegetal excrescences which distinguish the work of Peter Beard. The studio pottery and stoneware of Nancy Smillie (formerly of Wishaw but now working in Glasgow) exhibits some intriguing experiments with different glazes and the use of wax resist techniques to leave certain areas of the body exposed.

CLAY MODELLING

The modelling of clay into various objects such as figures or mantel ornaments was an old-established form of folk art in Scotland, as in most other countries. In Scotland clay was crudely fashioned into 'lame pigs' (lame being merely the Scots form of loam or clay). Whether these 'pigs' got their name from the yellowish colour of the baked clay or from the Gaelic word *pigean* (meaning a little jug) is debatable. Even now people refer to a pottery hot-water bottle as a 'pig' and in times past the term was often applied to any small utensil or drinking vessel of local manufacture. Arising out of this, perhaps, was a more specific

term. Small pottery vessels with a narrow slit for coins were used
as penny banks. These crocks were popularly known as pirley
pigs or pinner pigs and, by association of ideas, many of them
came to be fashioned like the porcine variety. Piggy-banks are,
of course, a universal feature of small savings and are not
confined to the thrifty Scots, but it seems more coincidental than
confusing that pirley pigs should allude both to the animal and to
the ancient Scots word for a crock. Pirley pigs of the folk art
variety were popular throughout the nineteenth century and
many of these primitive, unmarked pieces of folk pottery have
survived to this day. It is not surprising, therefore, that some of
the present generation of craft potters should have turned their
attention to the traditional pirley pig. Ian and Elizabeth Hird of
the Kelso Pottery have recently added this useful item to their
range of semi-decorative wares. A novel dual-purpose form of
pirley pig is produced by the Strathaven Pottery. The gaily
coloured pig has the characteristic slit indicating its function as a
bank, but by up-ending the animal and terminating his snout in a
narrow aperture, the piggy bank is transformed into an attractive
flower vase.

Purely decorative figures in clay consist mainly of animals,
such as those modelled by Elizabeth Alston of Edinburgh,
Castlewynd Studios of Inverdruie, Hugh Comrie of Alva,
domestic figures and Highland characters, such as those produced
by Orr of Lybster and Irene Morton of Minishant. The best-
known pottery characters, however, are the MacGlaurs (glaur
being Lowland Scots for mud or clay), a family of terracotta
caricatures in Highland costume, aimed at the mass market. In
similar vein, but with a more subtle brand of whimsicality are the
Odd Bods, modelled by David Evans of Fort William.

PAINTED CERAMICS

Tantallon Ceramics of North Berwick manufacture a range of
domestic wares which are rather pedestrian in form, but are
redeemed by the fact that their white earthenware body is hand-
painted. The transformation of quite ordinary wares by this
method is also practised by several artists who do not themselves
fashion the basic pottery or porcelain. Plain flat tiles are an ideal
medium for screen printing and excellent examples of this craft
are produced by Peter Deuling of Hamilton and Mynde
Ceramics of West Kilbride, the latter also using lithography and
hand-glazing. Mrs K.M. Black of Speyside Crafts, Newtonmore,

decorates tiles with on-glaze ceramic paintings, mainly featuring aspects of Scottish wildlife. The same techniques are also applied to bone china articles such as mugs, cups and saucers and egg-cups. A glaze is applied to the article after it has been painted and then lightly fired in a kiln to fix it. The most unusual adaptation of this technique is that used by Rhona Rauszer of Skye who applies candle-smoke to ironstone plates and then sketches scenes from island life with fingers and fingernails. Subtle gradations in tone and shade can be achieved by varying the intensity of the candle-smoke at any given point. A clear glaze is then spread over the surface of the plate and kilnfired to fix the picture for all time. Nethybridge Ceramics of Inverness-shire specialize in hand-painted crests and Highland heraldry on porcelain plates and plaques.

[18]
Printing and Dyeing

The decoration of fabrics by means of printing and dyeing is an old-established industry in Scotland, but as a craft bordering on the fine arts it is of very recent origin. Since the Second World War the various techniques of printing and dyeing have been taught at the major art colleges, in schools and evening classes and because the equipment and materials are simple to obtain and use, screen-printing, tie-dyeing and batik have become immensely popular within the past decade.

FABRIC PRINTING
Various methods are currently employed by craftsmen and of these block-printing is probably the simplest. In this method motifs are cut into blocks from a wide variety of materials including linoleum, suitable vegetables such as potatoes and turnips, foam rubber and expanded polystyrene. Relatively little use is being made of the traditional medium, wood, which was the most suitable material in times past when fine lines and great accuracy of registration were required. Today the emphasis is on broad sweeps of colour and a greater freedom of line, and therefore the coarser substances are more ideal. The printing from these blocks is done with oil-bound inks, pigment dyes or direct dyes and considerable variety has been achieved despite the extreme simplicity of the process. Block-printing is used in the production of a wide range of articles from small place mats and panels, cushion covers and napkins to larger items such as curtain materials and upholstery. Hand-printed wall coverings are the speciality of Robert Carfrae of East Linton. Similar techniques are used by Gillian Falconer of St Andrews in the decoration of all kinds of household textiles.

SCREEN-PRINTING
This method of printing, introduced to Britain from China at the turn of the century, has now been adapted to the more industrial

aspects of textile printing, but its craft application is closer to the original Chinese version and is now widely practised. In Scotland screen-printing is the most popular form of textile decoration and though many of its exponents ply their craft in the major urban centres it is a growing feature of the rural crafts also. As the name suggests, this technique involves the use of a taut screen of material – silk for the finest work, though cotton organdie or terylene lawn are now more frequently used. Screenprinting is basically a refinement of the simple stencilling process, though nowadays profilm stencils have largely taken the place of the cloth or paper printing shapes which were formerly employed. Combinations of colour, together with the use of fabric which has been previously dyed to provide the background colour, greatly extend the range of variations and combinations of colour which are possible and the subjects which can be reproduced in this manner are infinite. Not surprisingly, much of the textile screen-printing done in Scotland is inspired by the traditional Celtic or Norse motifs, though craftsmen are increasingly devising their own patterns and breaking away from the shackles of tradition.

Screen-printing is used by Alan Keegan and Jack Richmond of the Calary Workshop in Newtonmore in the production of place mats and decorative panels, the latter often hand or machine-sewn to form larger hangings. Screen-printed textiles are also among the products of the Melvaig Pottery in Ross-shire, the Stencil Studio Workshop of Beauly and Studio Seventeen at Balnakeil.

BATIK
Although silks decorated with batik patterns were known in Europe in the seventeenth century, having been imported by the Portuguese and Dutch traders from the East Indies, it is only within the past twenty years that this traditional craft of Indonesia and Malaysia has been widely taught in schools and colleges and has subsequently become one of the most popular forms of textile decoration. Actually this technique is not of Javanese origin, as is often popularly imagined, but is believed to have come to the East Indies from India in the Middle Ages and, in fact, there is some archaeological evidence to suggest that the technique was not unknown to the peoples of the Near and Middle East before the Christian era. The method of decorating cloth using a wax resist process is fairly widespread and has been

used in China and East Africa for centuries. Nevertheless it was in Java that the technique known as batik attained its perfection and from that island both technique and patterns have spread to the West.

For centuries hand-made batik was the prerogative of the upper classes. The ladies of the nobility in Java would spend months working a single piece of batik, much as their contemporaries in western Europe practised fine lace-making and needlework. Motifs were evolved which were analogous to Scottish tartans in their heraldic significance and a strict code of regulations was drawn up governing the wear of certain patterns. Others were invested with talismanic properties, guaranteeing health, fertility and prosperity to the wearer. Many of the traditional motifs were derived from nature or mystical elements, though the strictures of Islam prevented the direct representation of any living creature. The name is derived from the Javanese word *tik*, meaning a fine point. As batik operates on the wax resist principle, the design is drawn on the cloth using molten wax which is applied with an implement known as a *tjanting*, a form of wax fountain pen which requires great skill and patience on the part of the practitioner. Although the *tjanting* is still used for the most intricate work much of the European batik is produced with the aid of fine brushes. Both sides of the cloth have to be prepared with wax before it is immersed in a bath of dye. After drying successive treatments with wax resist followed by immersion in dyes gradually build up the complex batik patterns. Steam is applied to fix the dye and the cloth is boiled thoroughly to remove all traces of the wax paste. This traditional method, known as *tulis batik* (literally 'hand-painted') is seldom used in south-east Asia today. Various mechanical devices, introduced from the eighteenth century onwards, have transformed batik, and printing from special copper blocks known as *tjap* introduced in about 1840 speeded up the process even further.

The batiks produced in Scotland today conform in technique to the established occidental practice: beeswax, rosin and paraffin wax are used to achieve different effects. A similar technique is used in Nigeria using a starch resist and this method has also been adapted to batiks in recent years as an alternative to wax. Both starch and the different types of wax tend to crack in different patterns as the prepared cloth is dipped in the dyebath and this creates the distinctive forms of crackle which are a characteristic feature of batik. Far from being a blemish, crackle adds a new dimension to the decorative appearance of batik, creating marbling effects.

Batik decoration is most suited to small articles in silk or fine cotton, and for this reason much of the batik produced in Scotland consists of scarves. Batik silk scarves are produced by craftsmen of the Camphill Village Trust at Bieldside in Aberdeenshire and by several of the independent craftworkers, though the latter also make other forms. Irene Ryle of Munlochy uses batik as decoration to a wide range of small textile goods, Jane Foulis produces dress lengths in pure silk batiks and this is also a speciality of Inverhouse of Ardgay. Batik wall hangings are made by Sonia Stevenson of Nairn and Gunnie Moberg of Achahoish, the latter using Celtic patterns copied from the numerous stone crosses and slabs found in the Kintyre district of Argyll.

TYE-DYEING

Unlike screen-printing and batik, tie-dyeing is a process which has never been adapted to industry and may therefore be regarded as one of the very few genuine handcrafts. Superficially, it appears to be simple to the point of utter artlessness, and yet some surprisingly intricate patterns can be devised by means of cunning and skilful techniques in folding and tieing the fabric. Basically, the fabric to be dyed is folded or gathered in various ways and then bound tightly with raffia or rubber bands, though cotton thread is often used for very fine work. The fabric is then immersed in a dye bath and multicoloured effects can be achieved by rearranging the ties and immersing the cloth in successive baths of different dyes. By means of different folds and pleats, or the inclusion of various small objects such as pebbles, before tieing an infinite variety of patterns can be produced. While anyone can tie-dye at random and always achieve some kind of result it takes great skill and experience to formulate the right combination of folding, incorporating foreign bodies, and tieing to produce deliberate patterns of the desired quality. Marbling, geometric patterns and even complex floral or abstract motifs can be produced, the latter often involving various sewing techniques. Tie-dyeing is practised by several of the craftsmen already mentioned in this chapter.

[19]
Sheepskins, Deerskins and Sealskins

The use of animal skins as a form of protection against the elements must be as old as mankind itself and it is impossible to say at what very early date the hunters who inhabited the cold, northerly regions of Britain first discovered that pelts could be fashioned into serviceable garments. Bear and wolf have long given way to the sheep and deer and the principle has become infinitely more sophisticated though the basic idea of clothing oneself in animal skins is not so very different. Protectionist policies towards the North Atlantic grey seal mean that relatively little sealskin is now available to craftsmen and what there is has been confined mainly to small decorative articles rather than clothing, but a century ago sealskin jackets, trousers and gloves were commonly used by fishermen. The skins of rabbits and moles were also utilized until relatively recently in the manufacture of coats and jackets and the writer recalls, as a child, seeing the village 'moudie-man' (molecatcher) at work, skinning and drying the pelts of these little animals. Foxes and badgers both yielded their pelts to the hunter until fairly recent times and these skins were also made up into garments of various kinds.

The manufacture of clothing from animal skins was pursued as a cottage industry in many parts of Scotland until well into the present century, but has declined for a number of reasons — primarily a dearth of raw materials, coupled with a policy of wildlife conservation, and the advent of man-made substitutes. Moreover, the vagaries of fashion have played a not unimportant part in the demand for clothing involving animal skins.

SHEEPSKINS
As the supply of wild animal skins became exhausted, another source developed. The spread of sheep-farming from the Borders and Lowlands in the nineteenth century, eventually encompassing even the most remote districts of the Highlands

and Islands, had enormous repercussions, both social and economic, which are still being felt. Although the Cheviot and the coarse, long-haired Highland Blackface were reared mainly for their wool, the slaughter of sheep for meat also yielded a valuable quantity of skins. These were often sent to fellmongers to be de-haired and processed into leather, but a fair proportion of sheepskins remained in the Highlands and were transformed by primitive local methods into rugs and jerkins. For years sheepskin rugs were regarded as no more than a primitive luxury enjoyed by people who could afford nothing better. In recent years, however, there has been a marked reappraisal of the humble sheepskin rug and this has resulted in the development of a considerable craft industry devoted to the processing of sheepskins, mainly into rugs but also into small articles of clothing. M.A. and J.G. Blance of Skellister in Shetland, for example, specialize in hats and caps fashioned from sheepskin.

Formerly the crofters who cured sheepskins used to dye them in fancy colours to match the interior decor of their cottages. Although dyed sheepskin rugs are still to be found, the colours are much more muted than they used to be, with tawny shades predominating. The majority of sheepskin rugs now being made, however, are left undyed and the emphasis is now laid on the colours inherent in the fleeces of different breeds. Naturally, the white fleeces of the Cheviot and Highland Blackface predominate, with the occasional black or dark brown fleece among them, but other breeds provide considerable variety – the soft, fine fleece of Welsh black, the very soft, toffee-brown fleece of the Shetland moorit or the St Kilda mouflon, and the particoloured fleece of Jacob's sheep, with shades of white and cream splashed with brown patches. The magnificent glossy fleece of Icelandic sheep, with shades ranging from light beige to deepest black, is also highly prized. As a rule the fleeces are taken from sheep of mature years but the skins of new-born lambs which have not survived the lambing season are also pressed into service.

The process of cleaning and curing sheepskins is a lengthy one. Once the skins have been thoroughly cleaned and degreased they are left to soak in tanning tubs containing larch or mimosa bark, then washed again, stretched on frames to dry in the sun and finally brushed carefully to bring up the full luxuriant texture of the wool. Sheepskin rugs are widely produced in many parts of the country from the Borders to the Shetland islands. In Shetland, in fact, sheepskin products have now become a major enterprise and rugs and related articles in sheepskin and lambskin are exported from the far north by Laurence Brown of Vidlin, Peter Johnston of Bixter, Henry Sinclair of Bigton and the Reawick Lamb Marketing Company. Farther south sheepskin rugs are produced by A. and J. Sutherland of Occumster in Caithness, Viking Marketing of Beauly, Lindor Sheepskins of Rendall in the Orkney islands and D. MacPherson and Company of Elgin, noted for their 'Highland Fleece' rugs.

Balnakeil Sheepskins make sheepskin mitts and other small articles as well as rugs. Sheepskin articles are among the goods handled by Donald MacGillivray of the Hebridean Crofter-Weavers' Association in Benbecula, Waternish Blackface Sheepskins of Skye, the Harris Craft Guild, the Garve Work Society and Earra Gael of Tarbert, Argyll. Borshod of Inverness make sheepskin jackets and other garments, as well as suede and leather wear in general.

DEERSKIN

A familiar sight to this day is the red deer which are to be found all over Scotland from Dumfriesshire and the Borders to Caithness and Sutherland in the far north. Traditionally, the Scottish red deer was a forest dweller, but the wild moorlands of the north and west were denuded of their trees centuries ago and the red deer has had to adapt to an alien environment. The average red deer of the present day is a much smaller animal than his forest-dwelling ancestors, as their remains, recovered from peat bogs, testifies. Curiously enough Scottish red deer, introduced to the forests of New Zealand's Fiordland and Westland provinces in recent years, have regained their former stature and are now much larger than their Scottish contemporaries.

Deerskin has always been an important source of leather and hides, though the deer population fluctuated considerably in the past three centuries and for long it has been superseded by sheepskin as the primary skin for leather and skin products. Grogport Rugs of Carradale, Argyll, alone produce deerskin rugs today (in addition to their sheepskin and sealskin rugs, stools and cushions), but elsewhere deerskin is used for a variety of smaller articles. Deerskin Crafts of Jedburgh use this attractive hide in the manufacture of handbags, purses and other small goods, and similar articles are produced by members of the Garve Work

Society and Lochside Gems of Fearnan in Perthshire. Stobs Castle Products of Hawick use stagskin combined with wool in their range of deerskin garments. Two craft groups in Perthshire specialize in deerskin products, making handbags, key-cases, spectacle cases and purses: Perthshire Crafts of Dunkeld and G.B. Wilson and Son of Pitlochry. Deerskin lends itself admirably to the suede process and in this guise it is used in the manufacture of clothing, handbags, and small articles by Deerskin Crafts of Jedburgh. Sueded deerskin overblouses are also a speciality of Perthshire Crafts of Dunkeld. Cuams, belts, lamps, key-rings and even flasks are among the seemingly unlikely articles made of deerskin by Inveroykel Crafts of Ardgay in Ross-shire.

SEALSKIN

The comparative scarcity of sealskin nowadays has restricted its usage to smaller articles. Although Mrs Arthur of Grogport uses sealskin in rugs, other craftsmen have confined this expensive material to small articles, of which the miniature seals are the best known. The glossy, silvery appearance of seal fur makes it ideal for the more decorative items and it has even been utilized in sealskin jewellery, such as brooches, pendants, earrings, belts, watch-straps, dog collars and key-rings. Sealskin products, consisting mainly of these small decorative articles, but occasionally running to purses, hats and handbags, are made by members of the Harris Craft Guild, J.M. and G. Johnson of Girlsta in Shetland, Mrs Jean Sandison of Baltasound, in the extreme north of the Shetland isles, and by John Warner of Spinningdale on the Dornoch Firth. The usual range of sealskin goods are also produced by craftworkers whose products are handled by Viking Marketing of Beauly.

[20]
Silversmithing

The paucity of Scottish silver reflects both the poverty and the turbulent history of the country. Relative to England or the countries of western Europe, Scotland lacked both the natural resources and the industry to afford fine silver and goldsmith's work. What silver there was tended to be regarded as a form of money, to be called in and melted down as occasion demanded – and there were plenty such occasions between the thirteenth and eighteenth centuries. Because articles of silver tended to be more ephemeral in Scotland than elsewhere there was seldom much time or artistry wasted on unnecessary ornamentation. Thus there developed a simple functional style of metalwork which has certain affinities with the Bauhaus movement of the Twenties, though anticipating it by hundreds of years.

Scotland was not without its own sources of both gold and silver. Silver was mined in the Upper Ward of Lanarkshire from the fourteenth century and the extraction of gold and silver from the Lowther or Lead Hills which divide Lanarkshire and Dumfriesshire earned for this district the nickname of 'God's Treasure House in Scotland' during the seventeenth and eighteenth centuries when output of precious metals was at its height. Alluvial gold has been found in many Scottish rivers but has seldom been regarded as a commercial proposition. The best-known examples of Scottish gold work are the Honours of Scotland, the regalia of the Scottish kings now preserved in Edinburgh Castle, but there is a quite considerable amount of small jewellery, mainly rings and brooches, composed of Scottish gold.

Scottish goldsmiths are known to have existed as a craft body from the middle of the fifteenth century, but it is significant that they were too few in number to constitute a separate guild and, in fact, formed part of the Craft of Hammermen who also included pewterers, braziers, coppersmiths, armourers and blacksmiths. This absorption of goldsmiths into a guild devoted to the more mundane forms of metalwork probably dispelled any fancy notions which they might otherwise have had, but it also explains the functional attitude towards the precious metals. Moreover, there were very few patrons who might have encouraged goldsmiths to think of themselves as artists rather than as craftsmen. The more successful ones gravitated towards banking; 'Jingling Geordie' Heriot, goldsmith and banker to King James VI and I is always regarded as a prime example. The less successful, however, were content to ply their craft of supplying silverware to those who could not afford the more decorative (but also much more expensive) imported articles.

Scottish silverware tended to be regarded as something second-rate, often despised by the wealthier classes who preferred the extravagance of English and Continental baroque and rococo styles. Wisely the Scottish craftsmen never attempted to emulate these imports, but developed their own simple forms. As a result Scottish silver came to be distinguished for its smooth lines and simple shapes, of which the pear-shaped jugs and bullet teapots are probably the most characteristic. Emphasis was laid on plain surfaces devoid of ornament other than the occasional coat of arms of the owner. Not for Scottish silver were the extravagant flourishes and excrescences produced by piercing, fretting, chasing, gadrooning, repoussage or any other technique practised elsewhere in the seventeenth and eighteen centuries. There was a spirit of independence in Scottish silver of this period which makes it stand out, in retrospect, from the work produced south of the Border. Unlike England, whose gold and silver work was dominated in that period by craftsmen of Huguenot origin, Scotland's goldsmiths were not subject to interference or influence from any fashions beyond its frontiers. Furthermore there was scant evidence of any influence from Edinburgh affecting the craftsmen who worked in the provincial burghs. Although there were naturally more silversmiths working in the capital than any other town, the craft was conducted in every other town of any size and even in some, like Banff and Tain, which are relatively small even to this day.

There has been an enormous upsurge of interest in Scottish silverware in the past fifty years and this craft, so long disregarded, has been the subject of a marked reappraisal. In particular, articles bearing the hallmarks of the smaller burghs where silversmiths operated at one time are now highly prized. It is a matter for supreme regret that the tradition of provincial silverwork should have died out at the beginning of the nineteenth century. It was effectively killed by the Statute of 1836 which required all silver articles to be sent to the assay offices in Glasgow or Edinburgh to be marked. Previously assay offices had functioned in many of the smaller towns and when this facility was removed there was a logical tendency for craftsmen to gravitate towards Edinburgh and Glasgow where the great bulk of Scottish silver has been fashioned ever since. To this day it is the larger commercial jewellers and silversmiths in these two cities, and to a lesser extent in Aberdeen and Dundee, that give employment to the designers and craftsmen who graduate from the art colleges. By the middle of the nineteenth century Scottish silver had become completely submerged in the contemporary fashion for florid, ebullient plate. Having flourished for so long without regard to the styles and influences of other countries, it now went to the other extreme, and became thoroughly eclectic, drawing inspiration from Europe, pre-Colombian America, Egypt, the Far East, India and North Africa. These disparate ingredients were compounded with what were fondly regarded as Scottish traditions, which drew elements from the styles associated with the ancient Picts, the Celts and the Norsemen. Scottish silver of the second half of the nineteenth century owed much to the romantic revival associated with the works of Sir Walter Scott. This was the period in which the *quaich* was revived and transformed. Genuine quaichs were simple, shallow drinking vessels fashioned in wood or horn and very seldom in silver. In their 'Balmoralized' form they became large, clumsy silver mugs, over-ornamented with thistles and Celtic knots. The same penchant for the much-abused native floral emblem characterized many of the other silver articles produced in the same period, mainly as trophies and presentation pieces. This ostentation in Scottish silver was foreign to the age-old tradition and it has been a long time dying. The mere cost of the raw materials led to the decline of silverware during the First World War and the steady increase in the cost of silver from 1920 onwards has forced silversmiths to return to the simpler styles of the seventeenth and eighteenth centuries.

Economic necessity has coincided with the reaction against ornament for ornament's sake and the functionalism propounded by Gropius and his disciples in the Twenties was enthusiastically accepted in Scotland. Simplicity to the point of severity is the hallmark of modern Scottish silver whose beauty lies in form rather than surface treatment. Unfortunately the soaring cost of silver in recent years has seriously stunted the growth of the craft in Scotland, as everywhere else. For this reason most of the craftsmen who work in precious metals have been forced to concentrate their energies on jewellery where a little goes a long way and offers a reasonably quick return. Very few silversmiths can now afford to produce larger articles as a speculative venture and for this reason much of the more important silverwork today consists of specially commissioned pieces, both civic and ecclesiastical.

The exigencies of hallmarking have also forced the majority of the independent craftsmen to work in or near Edinburgh or Glasgow (though David Hodge, who works in Aberdeen, is a notable exception). Several other leading silversmiths work fairly close to the major cities and thus contrive to get the best of both worlds. John Leslie Auld of Thorntonhall near Glasgow works in gold, silver and enamels producing jewellery and special commissions, both domestic, civic and ecclesiastical. A.R. Angell of Paisley specializes in the more mundane forms of silverware, such as cigarette and snuff-boxes, tankards and quaichs (the last-named being much closer to the traditional vessels in style and decoration than their nineteenth-century counterparts). John Creed of Milton of Campsie in the hills to the north of Glasgow, makes jewellery and the smaller items of silverware, especially cutlery.

Trophies, communion plate, municipal centre-pieces and similar works commissioned by public bodies account for the major output of many silversmiths nowadays. Craftsmen engaged in this type of work include R.A.M. Dickson of Tayport, Bernard Harrington of Alyth, and Robert Stone of Garelochhead. Norman Cherry of Kelso also undertakes special commissions, and designs and makes ecclesiastical silverware to specific orders, as a sideline to his jewellery, though, like other silversmiths, he wishes that the balance of work could be reversed. The dichotomy between 'commercial' jewellery and the more 'artistic' silverware is one which shows little sign of narrowing. Electroplate has robbed the general public of its taste for fine silver as such and the disparity in price between sterling silver and silverplate is now so great that there is little hope of a fashion for more commercial silverware developing.

A few craftsmen have successfully bridged the gap by evolving forms of silverware which they can go on producing, with variations, for the commercial market. The most popular form of

Norman Cherry, the Kelso silversmith.

Miss Campbell of Plocrapool, Isle of Harris, using one type of spinning-wheel still popular in Scotland.

Stone-carver working in Scottish granite.

Curling stones manufactured by the Scottish Curling Stone Company of Inverness.

The late John Jamieson demonstrating his own invention—a loom warping directly on to the beam.

Annie McPhee of Skye weaving a Shiant rug.

Hand-made golf clubs by Ben Sayers of North Berwick.

Reynold Eunson of Kirkwall carving a Viking figure.

(*opposite*) Archery equipment by Border Bows of Kelso.

Modern and traditional methods of working with wrought iron at the studio of Bruce Weir, Bongate, Jedburgh.

silverware other than jewellery is the Celtic standing cross, modelled on the carved crosses of Iona and Kintyre with their elaborate tracery and distinctive circular segments linking the arms of the cross. These standing crosses are a speciality of John Forsyth of Alva, and are also produced by the Art Pewter Silver Company of East Kilbride. The latter combine silver with other metals, as their name implies, and this offers the other way out of the impasse created by the inordinate cost of raw materials. Malcolm Appleby of Crathes in Kincardineshire has developed a truly unique style of combining steel with silver and gold, exquisitely carved and chased. His chess pieces in this combination of precious and base metals, inspired by the famous Lewis chessmen now in the British Museum, were one of the attractions at the Exhibition of the Craftsman's Art held at the Victoria and Albert Museum in 1973. Norman Cherry has gone even further in his use of materials other than silver, experimenting with brass, copper and perspex. His candelabrum combining these unorthodox materials won a special award at the competition organized by the Saltire Society in 1973.

Roy and Alison Murray of Balbirnie produce all forms of jewellery in gold and silver incorporating precious and semi-precious stones, but also undertake commissions for silverware of all types and have found that this aspect of their work is now on the increase. Shetland Silvercraft of Wiesdale also make jewellery, but have produced a number of important commissioned works including the North Seven sea angling trophy sponsored by the Highlands and Islands Development Board. At the other extreme Shetland Silvercraft also make a wide range of more commercial silverware, such as christening spoons, napkin rings, desk sets and silver-mounted paperknives. Russcraft of Aviemore and Skipness Craft Workshops of Lochgilphead include silverwork in their repertoire. Margaret Shepherd of Barras near Stonehaven specializes in silverware using chasing and repoussage, while Colin Stephenson of West Wemyss in Fife make various small articles in silver. Interest in silver objects of vertu — small boxes, étuis, wine-labels and cigarette boxes in the main — is still in its infancy in Scotland, but the investment potential of these wares in inflationary times hardly needs stressing.

[21]
Weaving

The importance of weaving in Scotland may be gauged from the fact that Harris tweed and tartan cloth rank with whisky as the things most readily associated with the country in the minds of people all over the world. Hand-loom weaving has been an important cottage industry in many parts of Scotland from the sixteenth century, and though the materials woven may have altered over the years, hand-loom weaving remains to this day one of the truly rural crafts of Scotland.

The origins of the Highland tartans are obscure to say the least. This writer recalls examining hand-woven cloth in Bulgaria which bore an uncanny resemblance to Scottish tartan and it may well be that some type of check pattern was more or less common across Europe, wherever Celtic peoples with their essentially pastoral economy settled. That some form of belted plaid was worn by the Scots in medieval times is not disputed, and the Norse king, Magnus Bareleg, won his curious epithet from his having adopted the Scottish form of dress. It should also be borne in mind that a form of kilted tunic was a fairly universal garment in the Middle Ages. There is also evidence to suggest that tartan cloth was by no means confined to the Highlands, but unfortunately descriptions of Lowland dress, and the striped cloth of which it was composed, are too vague to be described as tartan. Even the name is not Scottish, but is derived from the French word *tiretaine*, denoting a coarse woollen cloth. How common woollen garments were in the Highlands in the Middle Ages is a matter for conjecture, since sheep-farming did not become widespread in that area until the eighteenth century. It seems more probable that chequered cloth woven from sheep's wool was more common in the Border country. Woven woollen cloth seems to have been confined to the families of the Highland chiefs since they alone could afford to run flocks of sheep; their humbler clansmen clothed themselves in animal skins and coarse linen, woven from native *cannachd* (flax). Linen-weaving was, in fact, a widespread occupation carried on in countless cottages up and down the country. It was often the principal occupation of the winter months (which, in the far north and west, extended from October till the end of April).

The switch from flax to wool began after the Act of Union in 1707, originally to encourage the import of English wool, but though the Scots were newcomers to the weaving of woollen cloth they rapidly caught up with the West of England and East Anglia. As these traditional wool areas of England began to lose ground in the nineteenth century, Scotland developed more rapidly and gradually established a reputation for the finest quality woollen cloth, a reputation which endures to this day.

At this point the division between tartan and tweed begins to appear. The fundamental difference is that the yarn used in making tartan cloth is solid in colour, whereas that used in tweed manufacture is composed of fibres of various colours. The latter type of yarn is then woven into plain cloth whereas tartan cloth achieves its distinctive character from the arrangement or *sett* of the various colours to make up recognizable patterns. Before the weaving of woollen cloth in the Highlands was revolutionized by the invasion of the Cheviot sheep the pattern and colours of the tartans were dictated largely by the availability of suitable materials for dyeing the wool – soft greens and browns were obtained from the leaves and stems of plants, yellows from the *crotal* (lichen) or bracken roots, purples from blaeberry or bramble and blue from the elderberry. The ancient clan tartans emerged almost accidentally, coinciding with the substances available in the locality occupied by a particular clan. These tartans, with their soft, muted tones, disappeared during the period when the Disarming Acts were in force (1746-82). During that period the only tartans which continued to be produced were those worn by the Highland regiments. The first of these, the Black Watch, derived its nickname (later adopted as the official title) from the very sombre hues of blue and green which composed its tartan. Many of the other military tartans, some of them in use to this day, were variations or developments of this deep blue and dark green combination, with the addition of yellow stripes (as in the Gordon tartan) or red and white stripes (as in the Mackenzie tartan).

When the ban on Highland dress was lifted in the closing years of the eighteenth century, sheep-raising was already becoming well-established in the Highlands and there was a great upsurge in the production of woven cloth. This was the period when most of the tartans of the present day were formulated and which reached its zenith in the 1820s when the pageantry associated with the clan tartans was assiduously cultivated by Sir Walter Scott and King George IV (at heart a Jacobite romantic). The mind boggles at the idea of 'Prinny' disporting himself in Edinburgh in full Highland regalia – complete with flesh-coloured tights – but this royal seal of approval was all that was required to make tartan the most fashionable cloth all over Britain. Queen Victoria, an ardent enthusiast for all things Highland, merely reinforced a fashion which was already popular. It is significant, however, that while tartan and the kilt became fashionable with the Highland gentry and the upper and middle classes of the Lowlands, it was not so prevalent among the lower classes of the Highlands. Certainly tartan cloth was used for the shawls and plaids worn by both sexes, but it is ironic that the kilt came to be associated in the minds of the Highlanders with first the gentry and later the tourists. The Disarming Acts had worked much more effectively than their legislators could have imagined.

The ancient tartans were woven by hand and required considerable skill and experience on the part of the weaver to produce the intricate setts. The pleasing arrangement of the colours was allied to a very fine quality of yarn, and it is hardly surprising that Highland tartan cloth should have formed a valuable commodity soon after the Act of Union permitted its export to England. During the lean years of the second half of the eighteenth century, however, the weaving of tartan declined within the Highland area itself, and the principal centre shifted to Stirling, then an important garrison town on the edge of the Highlands. Doune, Perth and Fort William were also important centres for the weaving of tartan cloth, but gradually the balance shifted again, this time to the Borders where the mechanization of the weaving industry soon forced the hand-loom tartan weavers out of business. Today the bulk of tartan cloth produced in Scotland is machine-made in the Borders. Significantly also, the greater part of the hand-woven tartan cloth also emanates from areas outside the Highlands and Islands. Within the Highland area tartan cloth is still hand-woven by several craftsmen such as Ken Dickson of Aviemore, Murdo MacLeod of Stornoway and the group known as Lochcarron Hand-Loom Weavers at Plockton. Though Lochcarron employ several hand-loom weavers in Wester Ross, their registered office is in fact in

Galashiels in the very heart of the Border woollen country and it is in that area that the other tartan producers are to be found, including Wellwood Weavers of Selkirk and Ingles Buchan of Galashiels. Tartans are also produced by John Grugeon of Peterhead and the Strathmore Company of Forfar.

Although tartan cloth is made up into a wide range of articles, from men's ties to plaids and travelling rugs, it is chiefly associated with kilts. As has already been mentioned, the kilt is a garment of great antiquity – the 'garb of Old Gaul' – but in its present form it dates back no farther than the Napoleonic Wars. In its original form the kilt formed an inseparable part of the *leine croich* (literally a saffron shirt), a voluminous garment consisting of up to 24 yards of cloth, held in place by brooches and a waist belt. Its only resemblance to the later kilt was in its intricate pleating; early prints of Highlanders show the skirts of this garment often looped up between the legs. The troops who fought under Sir Donald Mackay of Farr for Gustavus Adolphus in the Thirty Years' War were portrayed in the *leine croich* – with the addition of trews (trousers) of a similarly chequered pattern. As well as the *leine croich*, the Highlander wore a *feileadh* (plaid cloak) which also served as a blanket. It was worn around the body and pleated over the shoulder where it was secured by a plaid brooch. The lower ends were pleated and secured by the waist belt in the same manner as the *leine croich* and the lower part of the plaid thus resembled the later kilt also.

It was out of these two ancient garments, a cross between a toga and a sari, and involving as much expertise securing correctly, that the kilt eventually developed. Originally known as the *feileadh beag* (little plaid) – anglicized as philibeg – it was often worn with trews and it was not until the raising of the Black Watch after the Forty-Five Rebellion that the design of the modern kilt emerged, though the amount of material required was progressively reduced from twelve to eight yards as economy measures during the French Revolutionary and Napoleonic Wars. An even skimpier garment was produced in the 1820s to coincide with King George IV's celebrated visit to Scotland, and this substituted knife-edge pleats for the heavy box-pleats of the military kilt. The two versions have existed side by side ever since, and as the nineteenth century progressed the wearing of the kilt and other articles of Highland dress was gradually codified into the present system of Hunting and Dress kilts, with tartans to match. Kilt-making is itself an art. Today most kilts are manufactured in Edinburgh, Glasgow or Aberdeen and are thus outside the scope of this book, although it is still largely a handcraft. Outside the main urban areas, however, there are many individual craft kilt-makers in Inverness, Elgin, Fort William, Alexandria and Stirlingshire, and even one (Daniel Smith) as far afield as Dunbar in East Lothian.

TWEED

By passing the weft thread under two and over two warp threads to produce a diagonal line across the surface of the cloth, a type of cloth known as twill weave, or more simply twill, is produced. This type of cloth was stouter and more durable than the plain weave homespuns favoured in England and Wales and became a Scottish speciality in the late eighteenth century. In Scotland itself twill was pronounced 'tweel' and in the cavalier approach to orthography at the time, it was often written in this form. A clerk employed by William Watson of Hawick inadvertently wrote the word as 'tweed' on an invoice to the London cloth merchant, James Locke, in 1826, and Locke perpetuated the error when he ordered a repeat. In this curious fashion the world-famous Scottish tweed came into being. The fact that the river of that name is associated with the Borders is purely coincidental, but to this day there are many people who assume that this distinctive Scottish cloth derived its name from the River Tweed.

Today the best-known brand of this plain fabric is Harris tweed, a name which was the subject of a protracted legal battle some years ago and is jealously guarded to this day and denoted by the 'orb' trademark. But tweeds are woven in many other parts of Scotland and even across the Border in Yorkshire and Northumberland. Because of the tremendous variety possible in twill weaves – solid colours, heather mixtures, herring-bone patterns and checks – certain patterns, thicknesses and textures have come to be associated with various districts, although the basic technique is the same all over the country. As with tartan cloth, a great amount of tweed is now produced in great Border woollen mills, but a significant proportion continues to be produced by hand in the traditional manner. Nowadays the various processes involved in washing, dyeing, carding and spinning the yarn have been mechanized. In the old days, and even up to the Thirties in some of the remoter areas of the Highlands and Islands, these preliminary processes were carried out by hand, but today there are few people prepared to go to that trouble. The yarn is now mostly supplied in its finished form, though the weaving itself is done on hand- or treadle-looms. Even now, in this jet age, the only sound to disturb the peace of many a Highland strath or windswept island is the steady clacking of the loom located in a shed beside the cottage.

At one time the cloth was finished on the spot. The process of thickening and shrinking the cloth is known as fulling, and various methods and materials have been employed over the past two thousand years. In Scotland the cloth was thickened with soap and lye (stale urine gathered in special tubs for the purpose) and then tramped or pummelled in various ways. In the Highlands this process was known as 'waulking' and was performed by the womenfolk who pounded the tweed back and forward on a long trestle table to the accompaniment of waulking songs and *port a' beul* (mouth music). Afterwards the tweed was immersed in the running water of a stream to remove the fulling materials. Nowadays, however, the tweed is despatched to fulling mills for finishing by mechanical processes (which themselves date from the fourteenth century) and the ceremony of waulking the tweed is performed solely as a tourist attraction.

Hand-woven tweed is still very much a traditional rural craft in the Hebrides and the West Highlands. At one time it provided the only means of livelihood in wintertime for the peasant economy which depended on the seasons for fishing and farming. A certain amount of cloth would be needed for domestic consumption, but the bulk of it was exported to the mainland. Until fairly recently the bales of tweed used to be a very common sight on many a Hebridean jetty. Traditionally, the export of tweed from the Highlands and Islands was handled by middlemen known as 'tweed factors' who sent their agents annually to bargain with individual crofters and supervise the transportation of the bales of finished cloth to the warehouses in Glasgow, Greenock, Oban and other centres. Alexander Gillies Ferguson, a native of the remote island of St Kilda, left his home at the turn of the century to work for a Glasgow tweed merchant and, in the course of his duties, had the job of revisiting his former island home to gather the tweed woven by the St Kildans. Having successfully negotiated his first major deal he returned to Glasgow and resigned his post, on the grounds that what he could do for a tweed factor he could do for himself.

Thenceforeward he operated his own business and in subsequent years became a well-known figure around many of the Hebridean islands.

This spirit of self-help could never have existed in the bad old days when the crofters of the Highlands and Islands were utterly dependent on the laird, the tacksman (tenant farmer) or the factor (estate bailiff) for the import of manufactured goods and luxury items in exchange for the products of their toil. The pernicious system of barter, in direct violation of various government anti-truck acts, survived in the remoter districts and islands as late as the 1880s, and it must be admitted that the various mainland charitable organizations, founded to relieve the poverty of the Highlands, were often little better. A more self-reliant approach, however, began to develop in the early years of this century and this has since manifested itself in the growth and proliferation of such bodies as the Harris Tweed Association, the Hebridean Crofter-Weavers' Association, Highland Craft Producers, the Harris Craft Guild, the Garve Work Society and many others.

In particular, Highland Home Industries have exerted a great influence on the modern development of weaving as a craft, through the medium of their weaving school at Kilmuir in Skye and School of Crafts at Morar and, in particular, the tireless efforts of the late John Jamieson who has been largely responsible for the training of hand-loom weavers all over Scotland since the Second World War. Mr Jamieson was also responsible for many improvements in the design of the wooden hand-looms used by most weavers, and these are made in Dingwall to this day. At the present day the Weavers Workshop in Edinburgh's Royal Mile is stimulating the growth of 'craft' weaving and tapestry work by its periodic exhibitions and summer schools.

Tweed-weaving is probably the most prolific of all the Scottish crafts and its devotees far outnumber those engaged in pottery, the next most numerous of the crafts. It would be impossible to discuss in detail the merits of the various weavers individually and they are listed at the end of this book. In addition to tweed lengths, suitable for making up into garments, the majority also produce knee rugs and travelling rugs. A few, such as Russell Gurney of Turriff and Noelle and Arun Bose of Balnakeil, make patterned tweed cushion covers. Colonel and Mrs Innes of Marnoch, Aberdeenshire, produce smaller items, such as ties and shoulder bags, as well as bedside rugs and tweed

lengths, while Anthea Mill-Irving of Haddington concentrates
on men's tweed ties. Scarves, ties and girdles in hand-woven
tweeds are also produced by Mrs J.L. Polson of Baltasound, the
Achins Weavers of Lochinver, Veronica Togneri of Colonsay
and Bransby Clarke of Moffat. Several of these craftsmen also
produce more decorative forms of weaving such as place mats
and small wall-hangings. A few also make up tweed material into
ladies' garments, mainly skirts and jackets and that peculiar form
of Scottish tweed stole known as a *tonnag*. *Tonnags* developed out
of the short shawl worn by fisherwomen, but in its present
elegant form it has been changed out of all recognition. Susan
Searight of the isle of Jura specializes in decorative floor rugs and
wall-hangings which are not only hand-woven but also
produced from yarn which is hand-spun and vegetable-dyed on
the island.

OTHER TEXTILES
Mention has already been made of the linen woven in Scotland
from the Middle Ages onwards. Flax-spinning and weaving
declined after the Act of Union but the weaving of textiles other
than tweeds and tartans continued to be very important, and
linen was a major industry in many Lowland towns and villages.
Edinburgh was noted for its fine damask in the second half of the
eighteenth century, while Paisley and Kilbarchan in
Renfrewshire had a high reputation for their muslin and silk-
weaving. Shawls woven from the rich Kashmiri goat hair were
imported to Britain in the eighteenth century and it was not long
before attempts were being made to emulate them. Having failed
to establish flocks of Kashmiri goats, manufacturers came up with
a reasonable substitute composed of sheep's wool mixed with
silk. The earliest attempts at imitating the shawls of Persia and
north-western India were made in Norwich, but the Scottish
weavers soon surpassed these English attempts. In particular
Paisley became the centre of an industry geared to the production
of fine shawls distinguished by the repetitive motif resembling an
inverted comma, which was actually based on an ancient
Kashmiri fertility symbol. The industry was largely mechanized
in the 1840s, following the introduction of the Jacquard loom,
and thereafter the quality of design and production tended to
decline. Paisley shawls went out of fashion with the crinoline in
the last quarter of the nineteenth century, but what really killed
the industry was the competition from cheap printed cotton

shawls which were mass-produced at a fraction of the cost.

Linen and silk-weaving as a handcraft died out in the Scottish Lowlands in the middle of the nineteenth century. The rapid mechanization of the textile industry eliminated the concept of weaving as a cottage occupation, unlike the tweed industry which continued to rely on hand-loom weavers working in their own homes. The present craft of hand-woven silks and linens is therefore an entirely modern one, lacking the continuity which one finds in the manufacture of tweeds. As in so many of the other crafts revivals, this is due largely to the activities of the art colleges. The best known of the businesses in this field is Inverhouse of Ardgay in Ross-shire who produce a wide range of materials from tweed to silk and also make up these materials into skirts, dresses, blouses and other hand-made garments for evening and casual wear. K.A.G.S. Lane of Rockcliffe in Galloway works with silk and the finer woollen yarns, such as cashmere, alpaca and saxony. Mrs Kay Louth of Balvicar on the island of Seil weaves various types of cloth used in the manufacture of aprons, headsquares, scarves and cushion covers. Mohair is used extensively by a number of weavers, including Glen Cree of Newton Stewart, Hamish Murray of Camserney, Perthshire, Lochcarron and Hugh Galt of Barrhill near Girvan in Ayrshire.

[22]
Wood-carving and
Wood-turning

Centuries ago, when Scotland was more heavily forested than it is now, wood assumed paramount importance as a raw material put to a wide variety of uses. Apart from furniture and boat-building, wood was used extensively in the manufacture of numerous small domestic articles – boxes, containers, utensils and household goods of all kinds which, in more advanced countries might have been produced in pottery, pewter, copper or brass. The application of timber to furniture has already been dealt with, but wood extended far beyond the making of chairs, tables and bedsteads. It was used far more extensively in Scotland than in England in the making of domestic and agricultural implements, for example (and within living memory) the *cas chrom* or wooden foot plough, which was an indispensable tool in croft cultivation. Wood was an invaluable commodity in every occupation of the crofter, from arable farming to lobster-fishing and it also provided the material from which trenchers and platters, quaichs, coggies, bickers and luggies were produced on simple lathes. Spoons and spurtles of wood were also more common than metal flatware and wood was indispensable in the looms and wheels by which wool was transformed into cloth. Wood was prized all the more in the islands where trees were non-existent (at least in modern times). The carcasses of long-dead trees dug out of peat bogs or the harvest of winter gales on the great Atlantic beaches provided the islanders with an abundance of wood, often in an astonishing variety which might even include Caribbean hardwoods borne on the Gulf Stream and the North Atlantic Drift to a Hebridean landfall. John Sands, marooned on St Kilda for several months in 1876, noted that the islanders used bamboo found on the beach to repair the shuttles of their hand-looms, while the unique wooden locks which secured St Kildan houses were composed of exotic timbers which included Jamaican lignum vitae.

In many respects Scottish woodcraft differed in no way from that practised elsewhere in the British Isles. Indeed, as regards such crafts as clog- and furniture-making, the Scots lagged well behind their southern contemporaries. On the other hand, there were certain fields in which Scottish woodworkers excelled. Lack of ceramic, glass or metal substances forced the Scots to utilize wood more extensively in the making of the highest levels of workmanship. These utensils consisted mainly of cogs or coggies (resembling large buckets), luggies (beakers with a projection on one side serving as a handle), bickers (smaller beakers without handles, used as cups), quaichs (shallow cups with handles at right angles to the body) and mazers (bowls). Mazers are thought to derive their name from the Old German word *masa* (maple), since the burr of the maple was principally used for these turned vessels, the patterns and figuring in the grain of the wood creating a pleasing decorative effect. Wood-turning at its best can be seen in the splendid mazers of the fifteenth and sixteenth centuries, but understandably these are now extremely rare. As mazers formed the largest type of wood-turned vessel made in Scotland they were frequently ornamented, either with delicate carving round the lip and foot-rim or with silver inlay. A common practice was to inlay a large silver coin in the base, and examples with decorative silver bosses or roundels instead have been recorded.

Quaichs derive their name from the Gaelic *cuach* which signifies the depression in the centre of a bird's nest and aptly describes the basic shape of this shallow vessel. The earliest quaichs were carved from solid pieces of wood and had a relatively shallow depression within thick walls. By the seventeenth century, however, thinner and more elegant wooden quaichs were being turned on lathes. Like mazers they also had coins set in their bases and their lips were sometimes reinforced with silver or pewter mounts. The handles, projecting like lugs on either side, were often carved from the same piece of wood, but in later forms one finds them carved separately and joined to the body of the vessel, and in many instances metal handles were provided. The normal arrangement was to have a pair of handles diametrically opposite each other, but three- or even four-handled quaichs are not unknown. Quaichs were also made in horn, and when they were revived in the nineteenth century, were frequently rendered in silver.

Apart from the wood-turned variety, quaichs were often

produced in the same manner as cogs, bickers and luggies, adapting the techniques of hoops and staves used by coopers in the manufacture of casks. Coopering is an ancient craft which, once prevalent in every part of Britain, has declined sharply in the past twenty years, owing to the introduction of metal casks with plastic liners for beer and glass liners for wines. By 1950 it was estimated that fewer than a tenth of the number of coopers existed in the London area that had operated at the time of the Great Exhibition, and since then the number has dropped even more sharply. In Scotland, however, coopering is still a major craft associated with the production of whisky, which is best matured in casks. In 1968 alone, it is heartening to note that between fifty and sixty apprentices were started at the trade in Scotland, and in more recent years there has been no sign of this intake diminishing. The cutting of the oak staves over a slow brazier known as a cresset, and the setting of the metal hoops, are all intricate operations which require great skill on the part of the cooper, but they pale into insignificance beside the final task of shaving the inside of the cask until it is absolutely smooth — essential to discourage the formation of growths and bacteria in a beer cask. The use of the small inside spokeshave to achieve this silky smoothness is an art in itself.

Coopering was always an important trade in Scotland and it is hardly surprising that it was extended to the manufacture of smaller articles on similar principles. Tiny staves of sycamore and alder were cut, bevelled and jointed in the same way and fitted to circular bases to form cogs and luggies. The alder was immersed in peat bogs to stain it a rich dark brown colour — hence its popular name of Scots mahogany — whereas the sycamore was left uncoloured in its natural white state. Staves of alternate colours were used to create a striped or chequered effect. Though metal hoops were sometimes used to secure these staves, 'wuddies' (withies or willow strips) were much more common. The more ornamental forms of these vessels had sections of alder and sycamore built up in staggered formation like brickwork, but the most elegant examples of particolored woodware consisted of the so-called Jacobite snuff-boxes in which the alder and sycamore were combined in a form of marquetry to decorate the lids. Banding and segments of these contrasting woods produced simple but pleasing designs.

The advent of cheap earthenware or toleware in the nineteenth century led to the disappearance of coopered wooden vessels from the Scottish domestic scene, though the technique lingered on in more ornamental forms and enjoyed something of a revival at the turn of the century when cake caskets and biscuit barrels came into fashion. In recent years many of the traditional forms have been resurrected by Pitteuchar Woodcraft of Fife who produce spice jars and other modern wooden containers in addition to the characteristic Scots beakers of yesteryear.

WOOD-TURNING

The two principle methods of ornamenting wood by means of sharp cutting tools are turning and carving. The latter (which is discussed separately) is that favoured mainly by amateur craftsmen since it involves fewer basic skills and much simpler tools. Turning is a semi-mechanical process, however, which requires some kind of lathe and spindle on which the piece of wood is rotated. Primitive hand or foot-operated pole lathes were widely used until relatively recently, but nowadays the bulk of wood turnery is done with power-driven lathes. The actual cutting of balusters, twirls and baguettes or the gouging of bowls and beakers still depends entirely on the skill of the craftsman and the angle or intensity with which his chisels are applied to the rotating wood. In wood carving the design is also cut by knives and chisels, but in this case the piece of wood is stationary.

Although the mazer represents traditional wood-turning at its zenith, this technique was also applied to many humbler items. Bowl-turning was an important craft in itself and this lingered on, especially in the dairy-farming districts of the Lowlands, until the Second World War. As the need for wooden bowls in milk and butter-making declined, the traditional wood-turners began to turn to more decorative articles, and today there is a wide range of wooden hollow ware either in plain turned wood or with additional carved ornament. The same techniques are applied to dishes, plates and plaques, to lamp-bases, vases, barometer cases, table lighters, condiment sets, egg-cups, pepper pots and salt cellars, the components of imitation ships' wheels and other fancy woodware. The range of materials has also widened considerably – beech, mahogany, walnut, rosewood, box and lignum vitae being used alongside the more traditional oak and sycamore. Larger items include cake-stands, wall brackets and lamp-stands. The modern trend towards the greater use of woodware on the dining table has encouraged diversification into all manner of treen, from napkin rings to teapot stands, covered bowls and cheese-boards. Turned woodware is now produced by many craftsmen all over Scotland and it is one of the more popular lines in the craft shops. Domestic wood-turned articles of all kinds are produced by Stuart Keith of Pitlochry, David and Gillian Ferguson of Diabaig in Wester Ross, Johnscraft of Grangemouth, Katrea Woodcrafts of Newton Stewart, Kilmartin Crafts of Argyll, Murdo MacDonald of Leverburgh in Harris, Rhincraft of Kirkcolm in Galloway, Menzies of Dornoch, Scott Myles of Leuchars, Ornamental Crafts of Ulbster in Caithness and Stanley Whyte of Ford, Midlothian. William Hunter of Chapelton in Lanarkshire combines wood-turning with enamelling and copper etching in the production of a fine range of fancy woodware. R. Masson of the Woodturner's Shop in Brodie, Morayshire makes wooden bowls and other tableware, but also produces spinning wheels, stools, coffee tables and other small items of furniture.

WOOD-CARVING

The range of objects produced by carving is very much wider than that employing turnery alone. At one extreme are the sculptures and figures which belong more properly in the realm of fine art, and at the other extreme are the utilitarian objects which incorporate some measure of artistry, such as bread-boards, cheese-boards and butter moulds. Wood-carving in Scotland, as in most other parts of Europe, is an ancient form of folk art, though distinctive styles on par with the Welsh loving spoons or the incised stay busks of the English coast towns do not exist. Instead wood-carving was a prevalent pastime associated with certain communities and occupations, from the Border shepherds who sculptured the delicately curved heads on crooks and walking sticks to the fishermen of the north-east who made model boats. Among the coal-miners the whittling of stobs or wooden pit-props was at one time a common activity. These wood-carvers had one thing in common – a feel for the material inculcated over many generations and an almost instinctive approach untrammelled by any formal training in the craft. These ancient skills, transmitted from father to son, have almost died out, but here and there may be found men who produce sensitive carving out of the most unpromising materials.

Such a one is Donald Lowe of Cardenden in Fife, a coal-miner who has raised the traditional leisure craft of his calling to a fine art. He transforms odd pieces of wood and the branches of trees into animals, birds, fishes and human figures, the end-product being largely suggested or inspired by the shape and the grain of the raw material. In addition to his three-dimensional work, however, Lowe has created a new art form which he calls wooden portraits. Pictures are first drawn on paper and traced on to sheets of plywood; the drawn lines are then incised with a chisel and filled with plastic wood; the picture is coloured with wood stains; and the final picture is then lightly polished to enhance the grain and figure of the wood. The plastic wood acts like the lead in stained glass and prevents the different wood stains from merging into each other. Superficially the pictures may resemble marquetry although they are in fact conceived in an entirely different and original technique.

Trained wood-carvers do exist and there is now a flourishing industry in civic and ecclesiastical carving, though the bulk of this industry is concentrated in the larger urban areas such as Glasgow, Edinburgh and Dundee. Small church furnishings – communion plate, lecterns, fonts, offering plates and the decorative finials of pews – are produced by several rural craftsmen, including Stuart Keith of Pitlochry and Claude Gill of Arran. The more domestic forms of wood-carving include shortbread and butter moulds, in which the motif is cut intaglio into the flat surface of a soft wood such as sycamore. To the traditional thistle shape has been added a wide variety of motifs derived from Celtic, Pictish or Norse ornament and these forms of wood-carving have become very popular in recent years as tourist mementoes which also have a practical application. Among the carvers who specialize in these moulds and similar novelties are Colin Campbell of Longniddry, I.S. Clark of Blairgowrie, J. and I. Crichton of Braemar, John Crowe of Thurso, Johnscraft of Grangemouth and Schimacraft of Glenelg. G.S. Scott of Leven produces rolling-pins with thistle ornament, and various types of carved bowls, breadboards and ornamental desk equipment with carved wooden handles.

Many of these craftsmen also produce more mundane articles, such as house name-boards; but there is also a growing demand for hand-carved wall plaques, especially clan crests and other heraldic devices. Carved wooden plaques are a speciality of J.K. Scott Lodge of Cromarty and M.W. Stephens, I.S. Clark and R.A. Ballie of Rosemount near Blairgowrie Perthshire, the latter producing the full range of decorative panels and wall shields incorporating crests, coats-of-arms, regimental insignia and club badges. D. Riley of the Woodcarver's Shop in Cullen engraves wood-blocks used in the production of prints, but also concentrates on various forms of carving and sculpture and makes bowls and trays decorated with Celtic tracery. Ian Strachan of Aboyne carves relief panels and three-dimensional human and animal figures as well as sculptural abstracts. He also uses wood extensively in the manufacture of pendants and brooches and small objects of vertu.

Small boxes of all kinds were a Scottish speciality a century ago, produced in sycamore with black transfer prints of scenery and a covering of yellow varnish. This type of object is known as Mauchline ware, from the Ayrshire town in which it eventually became a major industry operated by the Smith family, but the craft of small boxes originated on the east coast in the middle of the eighteenth century at Alyth and was subsequently centred on Laurencekirk. These small boxes, carved by hand and painted in a manner said to have been imported from the Baltic area, are now highly prized antiques. Though Laurencekirk boxes were made by craftsmen working individually, the Mauchline ware boxes eventually became a major industry, with as many as 400 people employed by the Smith family under factory conditions. These black and yellow boxes finally became one of the pillars of the British tourist trade, along with Goss crested china and the comic postcards of Donald MacGill, but they died out just before the Second World War and have never been revived. Instead, small boxes, hand-carved by highly skilled craftsmen, are available from many craft shops though they are not closely identified with a particular locality as the old Mauchline boxes were. As such they have escaped the cachet of mere tourist souvenirs and many of them are exquisite works of art. In this genre come the carved money boxes made by John Crowe of Thurso and the beautiful carved boxes and chests produced by James Kirkwood of Pibroch Crafts in Crieff. Carving is used extensively in the decoration of jewel-boxes made by Peter Roy of Balnacra in Wester Ross.

MARQUETRY
The use of fine wood veneers to produce geometric, floral or scenic motifs was popular on the Continent in the seventeenth and eighteenth centuries, especially in France and the Netherlands. It is significant that the majority of the craftsmen

who practised marquetry decoration as an adjunct to cabinet-making in England were of French or Dutch origin. This attractive form of decoration, however, never seems to have made much headway in Scotland where craftsmen tended to concentrate on the form and line of furniture rather than surface ornament. Consequently there is no deep seated tradition of marquetry as a feature of furniture, although it has become immensely popular in recent years as a mode of artistic expression. Some incredibly detailed and intricate compositions have been noted in recent exhibitions, but marquetry is still largely a craft of the art school and the evening class and has not yet become commercially viable on its own. The lids of the jewel-boxes made by Peter Roy are frequently decorated with marquetry, while Commander M. Norman of Jamestown near Strathpeffer has a wide range of marquetry articles with the ship models and Highland dress accessories which he also produces. Recently Peter Roy expanded his activities and now makes chessboards and coffee tables using marquetry. One will occasionally find small examples of marquetry boxes and trays offered for sale, but the larger and more artistic forms of marquetry, such as pictorial panels, are seldom seen except in art exhibitions by amateur craftsmen. Analogous to marquetry is wood mosaic, but this seems to be confined at present to the heather root brooches and pendants discussed in the chapter dealing with jewellery.

[23]
Miscellaneous Crafts

The foregoing chapters have dealt with the larger and more important crafts but there are several minor crafts which are nonetheless making a significant contribution to the craft scene in Scotland. I have omitted any reference to the crafts associated with natural products such as perfumes and foodstuffs, though it could be argued that they are crafts in the strict sense and just as worthy of inclusion as ceramics or weaving. The domestic crafts of Scotland are, however, in a class of their own and are difficult to categorize in a book of this scope. The majority of them are derived from ancient skills which were necessary to the continuance of life at a fairly basic level – hence the preponderance of Scottish recipes involving oatmeal or ingredients which, in less thrifty countries, would not have been considered for human consumption. On a higher level Scotland is noted for its shortbread and although most of this delicacy sold in tins in the fashionable stores of Glasgow and Edinburgh is produced by mechanized processes, some home-made shortbread is available in various craft shops and other retail outlets in the Highlands. There are many different kinds of shortbread, varying in thickness, consistency and the subtleties of the particular recipe. Among these is the celebrated 'petticoat tails' – wafer thin fingers of shortbread with a delightful nutty flavour. The curious name is, in fact, a corruption of the French *petits goutelles*, one of the imports arising from the Auld Alliance of France and Scotland. Highland cheeses, mainly of the soft or semi-soft varieties, such as hramsa or caboc, used to be a common form of country produce, but this traditional craft has declined in the past twenty years. One may still sample home-made crowdie in Uist or Skye, but little of this distinctive Hebridean cheese is produced in marketable quantities. Heather honey is one of the more strongly flavoured types and not to everyone's taste, but clover honey is also produced extensively in southern Scotland. Jams and marmalades, including the more exotic forms flavoured with whisky, are to be found in many parts of Scotland, proving that there is still a market for home-made conserves to individual recipes.

Perfumes are a relatively new product of Scotland. The distilled essences of heather and other local flowers are produced by the Hebridean Perfume Company of Barra who also sell skinfood and other cosmetic preparations. Perfumes are also made by Diana Drummond of Lochgilphead and the Tralee Studio of Benderloch, both in Argyll.

CANDLES

Candle-making was an old domestic craft in Scotland, when every household would have rendered down tallow from the carcasses of animals and gathered beeswax to mould into candles. Cylindrical moulds for candles are made from sheet copper or brass and were once a common household implement. Cheap, mass-produced candles did away with the necessity for home-made candles and rush-lights long before the advent first of gaslight and then of electricity. Till recently, however, many parts of the Hebrides were not provided with electricity, so candles were a handy adjunct to the paraffin lamps which illuminated rooms. When I first visited Barra in 1959 I recall that the hotel in which I stayed furnished each guest with a candle-holder and a candle 'to light him to bed'. When candles were an indispensable necessity they were produced only in a strictly functional form; but in recent years the soft glow of candle-light has come to be appreciated as the ideal illumination for meals on formal occasions. Candle-light has romantic connotations which the harsh glare of electric light lacks. The association of candle-light with romantic or special occasions has thus inspired the growth of candle-making as a handcraft with some artistic pretensions. Many of the candles now produced are attractive in themselves and it seems a shame to light them and thereby destroy them. The more decorative examples incorporate many colours and are moulded into fancy shapes. Others, of the dumpier and square shapes, are often decorated with Celtic tracery in contrasting colours.

Fancy candles are produced by the Balnakeil Forge, who also make the wrought-iron candle-sticks and candelabra to match. Candles in unusual shapes are made by Highland Figurecraft of Culloden, and are also among the products of J. Hunter of Kinlocheil and the Findhorn Studios. Two firms specializing in decorative candles are J.I.P. Candles of Kincraig in Inverness-shire and Carberry Candles situated near Musselburgh in Midlothian.

SHELLCRAFT

As in other parts of Britain shellcraft was an art practised by gentlewomen in the eighteenth and nineteenth centuries. The ladies of the upper classes alone had the leisure time necessary to follow such an intricate and tedious pastime. Beaches were combed for different sizes, forms and colours of shells which were then arranged into stylized bouquets of many-petalled flowers, each petal formed by a tiny shell. In some cases a colourful effect was achieved by using as wide a variety of shells as possible. In others delicate shades of cream and white alone were used to simulate fine porcelain. These shell bouquets were encased in glass domes and were considered an elegant ornament for the mantelpiece or occasional table. Two-dimensional shellwork consisted of shell mosaics which ranged from purely geometric forms to landscapes and figural compositions. A great deal of time and skill went into the making of these elaborate shell pictures. At the other end of the social scale shellcraft was practised by seamen who assembled shells of different colours into pretty patterns and heart shapes as a primitive type of love token. These 'shell Valentines' frequently have brief mottoes of an amorous nature.

Out of this pastime grew the late nineteenth-century practice of decorating boxes and vases with shells on a wax or putty base. The manufacture of these shell-encrusted boxes began as an amateur pastime but soon turned into a commercial venture as the seaside tourist boom of the turn of the century got under way. Shell boxes then became a popular souvenir of the Clyde resorts, mainly associated with cheap musical boxes (the mechanical parts being imported from Germany or Switzerland), as well as jewellery boxes, needlework boxes and vanity cases. This form of shellcraft has survived to this day, though it has diversified into other forms, such as encrusted bottles, vases and lamp-bases. The quality of this shellcraft varies considerably, depending on the variety of shells employed and the artistry and ingenuity displayed in their arrangement.

Ornaments composed entirely of shells were another nineteenth century invention which subsequently developed into a souvenir industry. Shell ornaments ranged from the purely whimsical to the elaborately artistic and involved the use of the larger shells as the base or body on which smaller shells were arranged. Shells built up to form animal and even human shapes are frequently met with, though floral designs are also popular and in recent years more abstract arrangements have become fashionable. Shells are also used extensively in jewellery – bracelets, necklaces, earrings and brooches in particular. Shellcraft seems to have risen in status considerably in the past decade. Not so long ago it was dismissed as one of the more tawdry gimmicks of the tourist trade and as recently as 1972 there were no stand-holders at either of the Craft Trade Fairs who included shellcraft in their repertoire. Only two years later, however, there were no fewer than seven firms exhibiting shellcraft at Ingliston or Aviemore and the quality of design and execution in shell ornament seems also to have improved enormously in very recent years. Shellcraft jewellery and objects of vertu are produced by Cromarty Handcrafts, An Eilean Crafts of Rothiemurchus and Earra Gael. Martyn and Elaine King of Sanday in Orkney and H.R. Lakaschus of Opinan in Wester Ross are largely or wholly concerned with shell products. Two companies offering a wide range of shell-decorated boxes and vases, shell ornaments and jewellery are Glenelg Shellcraft and John o' Groats Crafts, the latter making use of the highly distinctive groatre and buckre shells found on the beaches of the north-east coasts of Sutherland and Caithness.

MODEL-MAKING

The making of models of various things is an ancient pastime which has developed enormously since the Second World War as working hours have decreased and people have greater leisure time to devote to hobbies. Traditionally, model-making was associated with those trades and professions which involved men in long periods of enforced idleness. Some of the most detailed ship models ever produced were those made by French prisoners of war in the early nineteenth century and it is not surprising that seamen in the days of sail often turned to model-making as a means of relieving boredom on long sea voyages. In Scotland, model-making as a traditional craft tended to centre on the ports of the east coast and today marine models comprise the greater number produced by craftsmen. Unlike many of the other crafts discussed in this book, model-making is often decried on the grounds that it is imitative and does not offer the same scope for free expression as pottery or wood-carving. The fact that models are often put to utilitarian purposes – for industrial or commercial demonstration or as visual aids in education – also tends to detract from their consideration on purely aesthetic grounds. And yet, beautifully detailed scale models of ships can possess the same attraction for the beholder as a work of art.

Model-making is one of the more widespread hobbies, with its own specialist literature, societies and exhibitions at both local and national level. For most of its practitioners, however, model-making is a leisure activity – an absorbing hobby which can sometimes be financially rewarding. The best ship models can, and sometimes do, command high prices, but when one realizes that a fine model may entail upwards of a thousand hours work, it cannot be regarded as the most lucrative of crafts. Significantly the highest prices for models are paid by fellow-enthusiasts who may lack the same degree of skill but can appreciate the labour and artistry involved. The general public, on the other hand, might marvel at the minute detail and intricacy of a model sailing ship, with rigging composed of human hair and tiny windlasses that actually work, but they would seldom be prepared to pay the four-figure sum that such a model deserves.

In such a situation it is surprising that model-making should have become a commercial venture at all. The secret lies in the production of standard lines and concentration on small models. Ship models are a sideline of John Grugeon's Scotscrafts of Peterhead, better known for knitwear and woven goods, and marine models are included in the products of the Scrieve Board of Fishertown. Craftsmen who have specialized in ship models, however, include Jack Priest of Scalloway who concentrates on the distinctive Shetland fishing boats, Rollo Kyle of Bishopbriggs who makes Clyde fishing boats and steam puffers, and Commander Norman of Strathpeffer who produces scale models of various ships as well as ships in bottles.

Ships are among the models made by Jack Topen of Longforgan in Perthshire, though his speciality consists of more mechanical models such as vintage locomotives and stationary engines. John Martin of the Reiver Design at Killin in Perthshire produces kits and model cut-outs. Donald McGarva of Balbirnie has moved on to model-making from furniture design and won first prize in the Souvenirs of Scotland competition in 1973 with his scale models of Scottish domestic architecture. McGarva has so far concentrated on seven or eight distinct architectural styles, ranging from the tower houses of the sixteenth century to the fishermen's cottages found in east-coast villages like St Monance. The models are built around blocks of wood over which are laid sheets of cork of various thicknesses and textures to simulate the smooth masonry or roughened stonework of the different kinds of dwelling. Windows, doors, chimneys and crow-step gables have all to be cut by hand, but this intricate and tedious job is justified by the superb workmanship of the end-product.

LAMPSHADES

Lamps themselves are a fashionable product of several crafts, such as pottery, wrought-iron, wood-turning, horncraft or shellcraft, and in some cases the craftsmen who produce them also make shades to match. More often than not, however, this is regarded as a separate craft resulting in lampshades of various materials, including copper sheeting, to hand-woven fabrics and printed linen, as well as the more traditional shades in parchment and raffia work. A wide range of lampshades is produced by E.M.R. Lampshades of Dalcross near Inverness. Patricia Ryan of Comrie, Perthshire, makes lampshades for ceiling, wall, standard and table lamps and also produces complete lamps. She specializes in the restoration, recovering and repair of antique shades and makes reproductions of period pieces. D.A. Evans-Teush of Fochabers produces woven textile lampshades, many of which are used by craftsmen potters who make the lamps themselves.

FISHING TACKLE

The Scottish lochs and rivers are renowned for their salmon and trout and angling has been a major sport for well over a century. Until about thirty years ago fishing rods were made by hand, but the process has now been largely mechanized and the majority of the rods now used are made in small factories in the major urban areas. Nevertheless, there are still a few country craftsmen making greenheart and split-cane rods by hand. One aspect of angling which continues to defy mechanization is fly-tying. There is an enormous variety of flies and lures, with exotic names like Greenwell's Glory, Zulu or Black Prince, designed to suit the vagaries of each month on individual waters and the fishes that haunt them. These flies are tied by hand, often by craftsmen with an intimate and proven experience of the locality. T.L.L. Morrison of Inverness engages in fly-tying as a subsidiary of his hornwork and plumecraft business, while Sutherland Fly of Wick produce all kinds of tackle for game- and seafishing.

[24]
The Craftsman's Dilemma

Although this book is primarily about people who make things it should be borne in mind that they also *sell* things. The main purpose of the two annual trade fairs is to put the craftsman in touch with the buyer, either wholesale or retail, who has the outlets necessary for the distribution of craft products. In many cases this provides the craftsman's only contact with the public who ultimately purchases his goods, but this in itself is not an entirely satisfactory arrangement. Quite apart from the vexed question of the retailer's mark-up, the indirect methods of selling seldom bring the craftsman the satisfaction of knowing how well his products are appreciated. Direct contact with the public is therefore something which most craftsmen welcome, even if it is only for the purpose of knowing that people with discernment and taste share one's views on the applied arts. In this lies the encouragement, if not the inspiration, which the artist-craftsman often needs.

On a more practical plane, however, direct selling to the public has obvious advantages over indirect selling through a retailer. The craftsman does not have to pay commission and – probably more important – is not kept waiting months for payment. Few craftsmen have the time or inclination to be their own salesmen as well. Increasingly the sales and distribution side of craftsmanship is being taken over by agents who act for a number of craftsmen, providing services more efficiently and economically than the usual indirect methods of selling. Furthermore, an increasing number of craftsmen are establishing their own showrooms on their premises, often combining showroom and workshop so that potential customers may see the craftsman actually plying his trade. Undoubtedly this technique is a powerful sales factor; there is nothing like seeing an object being made to stimulate the interest of the would-be purchaser.

This direct contact with the public is the ideal towards which many craftsmen are now striving. The snag about this, however, is that manufacturing and sales are disparate functions and time spent in chatting up a likely customer is time away from the potter's wheel or weaver's loom. Herein lies the dilemma of the craftsman who would like to encourage the public but does not want his output to suffer as a result. The self-employed, creative craftsman relies on five per cent inspiration and ninety-five per cent perspiration. Self-discipline is all-important and distractions, while welcome at times, are counter-productive. Even the interruption of a telephone call can cause a loss of man-hours far in excess of the time actually spent in conversation. Personal visits make the working day more varied, but they can be a very great distraction.

The following list of craftsmen, their addresses and their crafts is therefore offered with some trepidation. On the one hand, it is hoped that it will form a very useful reference guide to those who like to know something of the origins of a piece of pottery or knitwear; on the other, it is hoped that it will be used with some discretion and common sense. Not all craftsmen have facilities for selling direct to the public; a few may even have chosen a hermit's way of life and do not wish the public to beat a path to their lonely croft or shieling. If you feel impelled to make contact with individual craftsmen it is advisable to write in the first instance (remembering always, of course, to enclose a stamped, addressed envelope for the reply). Many craftsmen welcome visitors by appointment, and in this case a short telephone call will suffice. Not all craftsmen enjoy the doubtful benefits of telecommunications, but reference to Directory Enquiries will provide the answer.

Craft shops are a phenomenon of the seventies, and they are now proliferating all over Scotland. Obviously they vary considerably in scope and quality, both as regards the goods for sale and the degree of interest of the sales staff. Over the past three years I have visited every craft shop in Scotland and have found that while many are extremely helpful and knowledgeable about craft-made goods, others have been somewhat lackadaisical and it has to be admitted that some have been downright ignorant, neither knowing nor caring much about the goods offered for sale. No doubt time will sort out the good from the indifferent. The craftsman who is fortunate enough to have his work accepted by the Scottish Craft Centre is safe in the knowledge that his products will be handled by staff who are as courteous as they are well-informed – and, moreover, who have a genuine love of fine craftmanship – but the bulk of sales is in the hands of shops throughout the country which may well be relying on casual labour hired for the brief tourist season. Furthermore, marketing techniques are not (so far as I am aware) included in the curriculum of the art colleges and it has to be admitted that relatively few craftsmen have tumbled to the fact that clear labelling, if not packaging, is a decided advantage. Consequently the following list (Appendix I) may have the added benefit of identifying articles whose origins are somewhat wrapped in mystery.

Appendices

Appendix I
Index of Craftsmen

In the following guide craftsmen are listed alphabetically, with their addresses and code numbers indicating their crafts. In some cases where amplification has been deemed necessary, a few words have been added in parenthesis. Where the craftsman has a business name, the main entry is given under that name, with a cross-reference from the craftsman's name to the business name. This is particularly common in the case of ceramics and may be helpful in identifying the marks found on modern Scottish craft pottery. Agencies handling the products of a number of craftsmen are marked with an asterisk.

Code Numbers

1 Basket, cane and straw-work
2 Batik
3 Book-binding
4 Calligraphy
5 Candle-making
6 Copper, brass and pewter
7 Crochet
8 Deerskin products
9 Dolls and toys
10 Domestic crafts
11 Embroidery
12 Enamelling
13 Floral art
14 Furniture
15 Glass
16 Hornwork
17 Jewellery
18 Knitwear
19 Lampshades
20 Lapidary
21 Leatherwork
22 Macramé
23 Marquetry
24 Model-making
25 Musical instruments
26 Pottery
27 Printing
28 Screen-printing
29 Sealskin products
30 Sheepskin products
31 Shellcraft
32 Silver and goldsmithing
33 Spinning wheels
34 Stonecraft
35 Tapestry
36 Tartans
37 Tie-dyeing
38 Tweeds
39 Weapons
40 Weaving (mohair, silks, etc)
41 Woodcarving
42 Wood-turning
43 Wrought iron

Comrie Studio Pottery (Margaret Hancock), Dundas Street, Comrie 26

Connoisseur Reproductions, 39a Balbirnie Street, Markinch 14

Cononish Pottery (Janet Gladstone and Graham Noble), Tyndrum 26

Cook, Donald, Ward Farm, Kilbarchan, Johnstone 14, 16, 41, 42

Corvin Suede and Leather Co. (Paul Balogh), 6 Waterloo Place, Inverness 21

Coutts, Theodora, Commercial Street, Lerwick, Shetland 18

Cowe, K.M. – see Jacken Products

Cox, John – see Caithness Leather Products

Crail Pottery (Stephen T. Grieve), 75 Nethergate, Crail 26

Cranloch Industries (Clifford Jones), Cranloch, Elgin 9, 17 (nail pendants)

Craw Pottery, Lochranza, Isle of Arran 26 (majolica and terracotta figures)

Crawford, Elizabeth, Balbirnie Craft Centre, Glenrothes 35, 40

Creetown Gem-Rock Museum, Chain Road, Creetown 17, 20, 34

Creich Ceramics (Jacqueline M. Fraser), Migdale Road, Bonar Bridge 26

Crichton, J. and I., Braemar 41

Croft Crafts, South Neigarth, Sanday, Orkney 9 (masks and novelties)

Crofter Craft, Garve, Wester Ross 16, 21

Cromarty Design Workshop (Alison Dunn), Fishertown Craft Centre Shore Street, Cromarty 17, 26

Cromarty Handcrafts (J.C. McEwan), 11-13 High Street, Cromarty 20, 31 (acrylic paperweights)

Crowe, John S., 2 Bower Court, Thurso 14, 33, 41

Cullernie Crafts (Mrs O. Macrae), Annat, Little Cullernie, Balloch, Inverness 9

Culloden Pottery (Robert M. Park), The Old Smiddy, Gollanfield, Inverness 26

Cunningham, Ellen, 32 Mansewood Drive, Dumbarton 11

Dalgleish, D.C., Dunsdale Mill, Selkirk 36, 38, 40

Dalling and Henderson Ltd, 3 Welltrees Street, Maybole 21

Dalriada Crafts (Elizabeth Bridgeman), New Quay Street, Campbeltown 9 (character rabbits)

Davey, John – see Old Bridge Pottery

Fraser, J. — *see* Glenroy Horncraft

Fraser, Jacqueline M. — *see* Creich Ceramics

Fraser, John, 5-7 Market Hall, Inverness 17, 32

Fraser, Joyce M. — *see* Mairi Fraser Dolls

Frew, Hannah M. Craigielea, Chapelton, Strathaven 11

Fynecraft (Mrs J. Buchanan), Wood Cottage, Otter Ferry 13 (paperweights, plaques)

Gael Isle (Mrs D. Maclean), 69 Kenneth Street, Stornoway, Isle of Lewis 38

Galloway Lodge (Nigel Hesketh), 24-8 High Street, Gatehouse of Fleet 10, 18

Galt, Hugh and Sons, Waukmill, Barrhill, Girvan 38, 40

Gardiner, Adrian, Blackadder Pottery, Gifford 26

Garleton Fashions, 79 Abbotsview, Haddington 38, 40 (ladies' fashions)

Garson, George, 7 Newhouses Road, East Burnside by Broxburn 15 (stained glass and mosaic)

Garve Works Society, Garve, Wester Ross 8, 16, 21, 30

Garvie Enterprises, Kilmore, Oban 17 (plumecraft)

Gibb, Avril, Beech House, Skelmorlie 4

Gilchrist, John, 12 Ferry Road, Bothwell 17, 32

Gilchrist, R.P. — *see* Scot Art

Gill, Claude, Arran Gallery, Whiting Bay, Isle of Arran 14, 41

Gill, Michael, Jewellery Workshop, Whiting Bay, Isle of Arran 17, 20, 32

Gill, Stephen — *see* Arran Gallery Press

Gillies, Miss M.C.H. — *see* Catherine of Inverness

Gladstone, Janet — *see* Cononish Pottery

Glenburn Knitwear, 58 High Street, Hawick 18

Glencoe Ceramics — *see* Cononish Pottery

Glencraft Studio (M. Pritchard), Sheddon Park Road, Kelso 9

Glen Cree (J.H. Lochtie), Newton Stewart 38, 40

Glendinning, C.J. — *see* Burrian Crafts

Glenelg Shellcraft, Glenelg 31

Glen Folk, Glenara Cottage, Fort Augustus 9

Glen Lossie Knitwear, Newmills, Elgin 18

Glenmoriston Pottery (Peter Beard, Alan Nairn), The Smithy, Invermoriston 26

Hogg, Douglas, 34 The Square, Kelso 15 (stained glass)
Holden, Rozelle, Calderstone, East Kilbride 26
Holland, Tony M. – *see* Highland Line
Holy Loch Studio (Z. Predavec), Old Kirk, Kilmun, Dunoon 26
Howden, Jean, The Pottery, Muthill 26
Hunter, J. Uachan, Gleann Fionnlaighe, Kinlocheil by Fort William 5
Hunter, T.M., Sutherland Wool Mills, Brora 18, 38
Hunter, William J., 24 Main Street, Chapelton, Strathaven 6, 12, 41
Hutchison, Robert W. Woodside Industrial Estate, Kirkintilloch 6

Idrigall Crafts, Uig Isle of Skye 38, 40
Iglehart, Edward S. – *see* North Glen Studio
Illingworth, David and Lotte – *see* Far North Pottery
Illingworth, D.G., Dingwall, Ross-shire 38, 40
Ingram, Norman M., Sillyearn Grange, by Keith 9, 14, 24, 42
Innes, Col, W.A.D. and Mrs, The Old Manse of Marnoch, Huntly 38,
    40
Inniemore Pottery (Ann Baxter), Inniemore Lodge, Pennyghael, Isle of
    Mull 26
Invergyle Jewellery (Glen K. Frame), 5 Ireland Street, Carnoustie 17,
    32
Inverhouse (Mrs J. Richardson), Gledfield, Ardgay 11, 36, 38, 40 (also
    silk-dyeing)
Inveroykel Crafts (John Small), Inveroykel Lodge by Ardgay 8, 30
Islandwear, Hamnavoe, Shetland 18
Islay Pottery, Storakaig, Bridgend, Isle of Islay 26
Isle of Cumbrae Pottery (Donald S. Swan), Millport, Isle of Cumbrae
    26
Isle of Lewis Knitwear, Lochs Road, Stornoway 18
Isle of Lewis Pottery, 5 Hacklete, Great Bernera, Lewis
Isle of Sanday Knitters, Newholm Schoolhouse, Sanday, Orkney 7, 18

Jack, M. and J., Bowmount Street, Kelso 18
Jacken Products (K.M. Cowe, A.J. Greig), 81 St Peter Street,
    Peterhead 17, 21, 34
Jean Jack Art and Craft, 33 Stratherrick Road, Inverness 5, 13, 18
Jeffs, J.G., The Yellow Door, 9 High Street, Kirkcudbright 4, 40, 41
Jenny A'Things (Irene D. Mackenzie), High Orchard, Beith 9 (also
    draught excluders)

Lakaschus, H.R., Opinan, Laide, by Achnasheen 31

Lambert, Eva, Carnoch, Hallin, Isle of Skye 40 (Handspun and woven rugs)

Lamlash Pottery (Lindsay H. Hamilton), 10 Park Terrace, Lamlash, Isle of Arran 26

Lane, John, Allt Daraich, Sligachan, Portree, Isle of Skye 42

Lane, K.A.G.S., Rockliffe, Dalbeattie 40

Lapidary Workshops, Garlogie School, Skene 20, 34

Larbert Pottery (Barbara Davidson), Muirhall Farm, Labert 26

Largo Pottery (Anne Lightwood), Main Street, Lower Largo 26

Larissa Knitwear, Hall Street, Galashiels 18

Laurenson, Pat – see Glen Tanar Pottery

Lawrie, A.A. – see Starkit

Layton, Peter – see Morar Pottery

Leah Craft (C.J. Burton), 28 South College Street, Elgin 13, 41, 42

Leckie, Alexander, Garrell Mill House, Tak-ma-Doon Road, Kilsyth 26

Leighton, A., M. and M. – see Highland Products

Leighton, A.G. – see Lochside Gems

Leiper, W.R. – see Lapidary Workshops

Leman, John, Meikle Kinord, Dinnet 12, 17

Lephen Beag Studios, Torrisdale, Carradale 12, 17, 26, 27

Levien, C.J. – see Moray Firth Design

Lightwood, Anne – see Largo Pottery

Lindor Sheepskins, Braevilla, Rendall, Orkney 30

Linton Wall Coverings (Robert Carfrae), The Old Mill, East Linton 28

Littlejohn, Joyce, 12 Sruthan, by Scarinish, Isle of Tiree 12

Lochardil Plastics (Roland Hill), 12 Achvraid Road, Inverness 6 (clan crests)

Lochcarron Products, Waverley Mills, Galashiels 36, 38, 40

Loch Erisort Woollens, Stornoway, Isle of Lewis 18

Lochhead, Ken, Elwyn, Gorebridge 27

Lochhead, Thomas – see Old Mill Pottery

Lochmaben Handcrafts (May Roberts), Bruce Street, Lochmaben, Lockerbie 7, 18 (Sanquhar gloves)

Lochside Gems (A.G. Leighton), Fearnan, Lochtayside 8, 21

Lochtayside Crafts (Raymond Morris), The Old Mill, Acharn, Aberfeldy 21

McLellan, Margaret E.C., Hinaidi, Achintore Road, Fort William 11, 40

MacMillan, D.M., Gate Lodge, Torlundy, Fort William 43

McNaught, Sheila, Tullo-Cambus, Kilmahog, Callander 26

Macrae Mrs O.M. – *see* Cullernie Crafts

McVitie, Graham, Tynehead Cottages, Tynehead, Pathead 26

McWhinney, Liz, Reyflat Farm Cottage, nr Rosemarkie 35, 40

Magnus Maximus, 147 High Street, Fort William 17, 20, 32, 34

Main, William, 9 West Port, Dunbar 21

Mairi Fraser Dolls (Joyce M. Fraser), 18 Bishop Street, Rothesay, Bute 9

Maitland, Lady Jean, Reswallie, Forfar, Angus 11

Maka Knitwear, Commercial Street, Lerwick, Shetland 18

Malin Workshop (R. and M. Hedderwick), Monzie Square, Fort William 27

Mann, Denis, F., 14 Ackergill Street, Wick 15

Marine Handweavers, Portree, Isle of Skye 38, 40

Marroney, P. – *see* West Port Gems

Marshall, D., Balnakeil Crafts Centre, Durness 43

Marshall, Robert, Gateside Smithy, 20 Main Road, Gateside, Beith 43

Martin, E., Closeburn, Thornhill 43

Martin, Felice, 8 Treemains Road, Whitecraigs, Renfrewshire 1, 11

Masson, R., Brodie, Forres 14, 33, 42

Masterson, Luke, 9 Kip Avenue, Inverkip 17, 32

Matthews of Leslie (Roy L. Matthlews), 17 Westgate, Leslie 11, 39, 43

Melvaig Pottery, The School, Melvaig, Wester Ross 26, 28

Menzies Craft, Station Square, Dornoch 6, 12, 41, 42, 43

Metal Crafts, Claggan Road, Fort William 43

Michie, Alan – *see* Saxony Handloom Co.

Middleton Leather Co., 87 Bongate, Jedburgh 8, 21, 30

Miles, David and Janet – *see* Scarista Studio

Miller, John – *see* Ferryport Pottery

Mill-Irving, Anthea – *see* NIK Ties

Minchin, D. – *see* Waternish Blackface Sheepskins

Mitchell, James, Mitchell's Close, Haddington 40

Mitchell, Joyce – *see* Agate and Pebblecraft

M.J. Design (J.B. Youseman), 241 Main Street, East Calder 1, 14

Moberg, Gunnie, Ellary Farm, Achahoish, Lochgilphead 2 (wall-hangings)

Nethybridge Ceramics (Mr and Mrs J.N. Tenneroni), Station Road, Nethybridge 26 (clan crests)

Newbery, A.G.F. – *see* Skipness Craft Workshops

Newcraft (K. Newhouse), Carnbo, Kinross 6, 17

NIK Ties, (Anthea Mill-Irving), 27 Lethan Mains, Haddington 28

Nisbet, Peggy, Guards Road, Cheviot View, Coldstream 9

Nobbs, Brian, Findhorn Studios, Pine Ridge, Findhorn Bay 26

Noble, Graham – *see* Cononish Pottery

Norman, Cdr M., Tormod, Jamestown, Strathpeffer 21, 23, 24, 39

Norris, K. and P. (jewellery) – *see* Robert Cleary

Norscot Distributors (A.V. Normand), Grove Road, Kemnay, Inverurie 27

North Glen Studio (Edward S. Iglehart), Palnackie, Castle Douglas 15

Northpoint Graphics, 24 Mayfield High Street, Dingwall 27

Oban Glass, Lochavullin Estate, Oban 15

Oban Knitwear, Lochavullin Estate, Oban 18

Old Bridge Pottery (John Davey), Bridge of Dee, Castle Douglas 26

Old Croft House, 11a Orinsay, Lochs, Isle of Lewis 26, 27

Old Mill Pottery (Thomas Lochhead), Millburn Street, Kirkcudbright 26

Old Rectory Design, Cullipool, Isle of Luing 27

Orcadian Stone Co, (Donald Shelley), Main Street, Golspie 17, 20, 34

Orkney Knitwear, Junction Road, Kirkwall, Orkney 28

Ornamental Crafts, Hawthornbank, Ulbster, Caithness 6, 41, 42, 43

Orr Ceramics (Charles Orr), Lybster Pottery, Lybster, Caithness 26

Ortak Silvercraft (Malcolm S. Gray), Mount Drive, Kirkwall, Orkney 17, 32

Park, Robert M. – *see* Culloden Pottery

Pass, Norman – *see* Stobs Castle Stag Products

P.A.T.S 90 King Duncan Road, Raigmore, Inverness 7

Peebles Pottery (Jack Dawson, Bill Edmond), 9 Eastgate, Peebles 26

Pentland Copper Craft (Robert J. Mackay), 32 West Street, Penicuik 6

Perthshire Crafts, The Ell Shops, Dunkeld 8, 34

Perthshire Paperweights, 14 Comrie Street, Crieff 15

Peters, Ross – *see* Ross Pottery

Philip, R. – *see* Speyside and Cairngorm Sportswear

Starkit (A.A. Lawrie), Station Road, Kingskettle 17

Stein, Florence C., 5 Knowepark Village, West Calder 7

Stencil Studio Workshop, Old Railway Station, Beauly 27, 28

Stephens, M.W., Buttery Bank, Rosemount, Blairgowrie 41 (heraldic shields)

Stephenson, Colin, West Wemyss, Fife 27, 32

Stevens, Gordon, Mansfield, Maddiston Road, Brightons, Falkirk 17, 32

Stevens, June, Lentranhill, Lentran, Inverness 27

Stevenson, S.C. – *see* Caledonian Crafts

Stevenson, Sonia, Comrie Villa, The Links, Nairn 2

Stewart, George, Pitairlie Smithy, Newbigging, by Broughty Ferry 43

Stobs Castle Stag Products (Norman Pass), Stobs Castle, Hawick 8, 18, 40

Stollery, Ernest W.R., Lapidary Workshop, 14½ Sandend, Portsoy 17, 20, 34

Stollery, Janet F., Silver Workshop, 22 Seafield Street, Cullen 17, 32

Stone House, The (R.H. Henderson), Avoch, Ross-shire 20, 34

Stone, Robert, Woodburn, Portincaple, Garelochhead 32

Storer, Jean C. – *see* Spindrift Toys

Stornoway Pottery, 27 Benside, Laxdale, Stornoway, Isle of Lewis 26

Strachan, Ian, 2 Bellwood Road, Aboyne 16, 17, 41

Strathaven, Pottery, Strathaven, Lanarkshire 26

Strathdon Pottery (Zelda Mowat), Heugh-head, Strathdon 26

Strathearn Glass Co., 15 Muthill Road, Crieff 15

Strathie, C.S. – *see* Tayside Potters

Strathleven Knitwear, Lomond Industrial Estate, Alexandria 18

Stromecraft (Geoff Salt), Holly Cottage, Strome Ferry, Wester Ross 12

Struie Crafts, Aultnamain, Edderton, Tain 9

Stuart, Jessie, 117 Land Street, Keith 9

*Stuart McGregor Agencies, Glenorchy House, Dunira Street, Comrie 15

Stuart, Margaret, Burrastow House, Walls, Shetland 18

Stuart of Inverness Ltd, Cashmere House, Harbour Road, Inverness 18

Studio Salix, Salix House, Banavie, Fort William 27

Studio Seventeen, Balnakeil Crafts Centre, Durness 27, 28 (also photography)

Sutherland, A. and J., Moorings, Occumster, Caithness 26, 30

Organizations, Communities

and Craft Centres

Balbirnie Craft Centre, Balbirnie House, Glenrothes, Fife

Balnakeil Crafts Centre, Balnakeil, Durness, Sutherland

Camphill Village Trust, Newton Dee Community, Bieldside, Aberdeen

Dry Stone Walling Association, Gatehouse of Fleet, Galloway

Findhorn Studios, Pine Ridge, Findhorn Bay, Forres

Harris Tweed Association, Station Square, Inverness

Highland Home Industries, 94 George Street, Edinburgh EH2 3DQ (headquarters and main showroom; retail shops in Aberdeen, Elgin, Fort Augustus, Gairloch, Glenesk, Golspie, Iona, Lochboisdale, Morar, Strathpeffer, Ullapool and Poolewe).

Highlands and Islands Development Board, Bridge House, Bank Street, Inverness

Lewis Craft Association, County Buildings, Stornoway, Isle of Lewis

Marketing Association of Scotland, 543 Gorgie Road, Edinburgh

Scottish Crafts Centre, Acheson House, 140 Canongate, Edinburgh EH8 8DD

Scottish Design Centre, 72 St Vincent Street, Glasgow

Scottish National Institution for the War-blinded, Linburn Training Centre, Wilkieston, Ratho, Midlothian

Small Industries Council for Rural Areas of Scotland, 27 Walker Street, Edinburgh, EH3 7HZ

Weavers Workshop, Monteith House, High Street, Edinburgh

Museums featuring Scottish Crafts

The principal museums of Scotland all have fine, representative collections of the applied and decorative arts, with perhaps an emphasis on pottery, tapestry, silver and objects of vertu. The art galleries and museums of the four major cities have an active policy regarding acquisitions of the best of contemporary craftsmanship, with a bias towards the 'fine arts' of ceramic sculpture and tapestry. At the other end of the scale the many burgh museums, from Dumfries and Kirkcudbright in the south to Wick and Thurso in the far north, often focus attention on crafts, both past and present, associated with the locality. These burgh museums vary considerably in scope and quality, but they are invariably worth a visit. The chief museums are listed below, in alphabetical order by town. Details regarding burgh museums may be obtained from the Tourist Information Office in each town or district.

ABERDEEN: Aberdeen Art Gallery and Museum, Schoolhill, Aberdeen
DUNDEE: City Art Gallery and Museum, Albert Square, Dundee
EDINBURGH: National Museum of Antiquities, Queen Street, Edinburgh 2
  Royal Scottish Museum, Chambers Street, Edinburgh 1
GLASGOW: Art Gallery and Museum, Kelvingrove, Glasgow G3
  Hunterian Museum, Glasgow University, Glasgow G11
  The People's Palace, Glasgow Green, Glasgow G1

In addition to the burgh museums and the major civic museums and art galleries, there are several regional museums devoted specifically to aspects of rural life and industry.

FORT WILLIAM: West Highland Museum
INVERARAY: Museum of Farming Life, Auchindrain
KILBARCHAN: Weaver's Cottage
KINGUSSIE: Am Fasgadh Folk Museum
LEWIS: Black House, Barvas

NORTH UIST: Croft Museum
OBAN: Argyll Historical Centre
ORKNEY: Tankerness House Museum, Kirkwall
SHETLAND: Croft Museum, Voe, Dunrossness
    Shetland County Museum, Lerwick
SKYE: Kilmuir Croft Museum
    Three Chimneys Museum, Colbost, Dunvegan
SOUTH UIST: Croft Museum, Eochar
TAIN: Castlebrae Museum
THURSO: Folk Museum, Traill Street
ULLAPOOL: Loch Broom Museum
WICK: Auckengill Museum, Keiss